Reality Calling

The Story of a Principal's First Semester

Nicholas J. Pace

ROWMAN & LITTLEFIELD EDUCATION
A division of
ROWMAN & LITTLEFIELD
Lanham • Boulder • New York • Toronto • Plymouth, UK

Published by Rowman & Littlefield Education
A division of Rowman & Littlefield
4501 Forbes Boulevard, Suite 200, Lanham, Maryland 20706
www.rowman.com

10 Thornbury Road, Plymouth PL6 7PP, United Kingdom

British Library Cataloguing in Publication Information Available

Library of Congress Cataloging-in-Publication Data

Pace, Nicholas J.
Reality calling : the story of a principal's first semester / Nicholas J. Pace..
pages cm
Includes bibliographical references.
ISBN 978-1-4758-0047-0 (cloth : alk. paper) — ISBN 978-1-4758-0048-7 (pbk. : alk. paper) — ISBN 978-1-4758-0049-4 (electronic) 1. First year school principals—United States—Case studies. 2. High school principals—United States—Case studies. 3. School year—United States—Case studies. I. Title.
LB2831.92.P35 2013
371.2'012—dc23
2013022177

Printed in the United States of America

For Roxanne—the one thing I know for sure.

Contents

Acknowledgments   vii

Preface   ix

Introduction   xi

1   March: Looking to Lead   1

2   June: Moving On   9

3   July: First Impressions   17

4   August: Laying a Foundation   25

5   Mid-August: Here Come the Teachers   33

6   Late August: There's Nothing Like the First Day of School   43

7   Early September: Baptism by Fire   55

8   Mid-September: Searching for Rhythm   63

9   Mid-September: D-Day   81

10   Early October: The Unusual Is Routine   87

11   Mid-October: Definitions and Personalities   99

12   Late October: Stepping Forward, Stepping Back, Staying Even?   111

13   Homecoming: Black, White, and Gray   121

14   Early November: Fights, Fatigue, Poems, and Prayers   135

15   Mid-November: The Media, the Mentee, the Abyss, and the Bandit   147

16   December: A Better Way?   161

17 Mid-December: Looking Back, Looking Ahead   173

References   187

Acknowledgments

I owe many people a debt of gratitude for their assistance with this project. I thank Tom Koerner of Rowman & Littlefield Education for seeing the value in addressing the challenges and opportunities of the principalship in this unique format. He, Caitlin Crawford, and Patricia Stevenson are first-class professionals.

Many current and former school administrators, attorneys, psychologists, and parents shared ideas, experiences, and suggestions in the development of this work. They are too numerous to mention here, but they know who they are. They have my admiration and gratitude for their assistance with this project, but more importantly for the work they do.

In the fall of 2012, Jeff Dieken, Troyce Fisher, Steve Foster, Betty Hogan, and Dewitt Jones served as expert readers of a very rough initial draft. They, along with students enrolled in the 2012 All-Iowa Principalship Cohort at the University of Northern Iowa, provided insightful feedback. Writing group partners Gowri Betrabet Gulwadi, Mary Frisbee Johnson, and Marybeth Stalp helped shape the three principals' characters. Betty Hogan and Deborah J. Gallagher turned my attention to many subtleties I was likely to miss, and John K. Smith was always up for reading yet another draft. Finally, Roxanne, Sienna, and Adison Pace have contributed in ways that can never be explained.

Preface

Several years ago, I was in the throes of writing my doctoral dissertation, which examined the school experiences of eight young people who were openly gay or lesbian in high school. A large part of the dissertation and subsequent book (Pace, 2009) were students' accounts of the ways they navigated high school. In the midst of trying to effectively share their fascinating stories, my friend and mentor John K. Smith said something simple that has stuck with me: "Stories are what move us."

Since that time, I have tried to apply that truth to the way I teach. Sometimes it means telling a story that happened to me as principal. At other times it involves a case study, guest speaker, or re-creating a unique scenario through role-play (Pace, 2011). The goal is always to move beyond statistics, charts, and the so-called science of school leadership to illuminate real people's leadership efforts under less-than-sterile textbook circumstances. This work of fiction is my latest effort to do so.

Three overarching goals drove its creation. First, I sought to illustrate the fact that *nothing* is off the table in terms of what might come through the principal's door at any moment. In fact, nearly every time I spoke with principals while writing this book, they shared rich stories that might sound outlandish to many but are fairly unremarkable or routine to other principals. Second, I wanted to caution new principals against feeling as though they should possess all of the answers. As a new principal, I was struck by the way people expected me to have the answers because I held the title. I know I didn't do a good enough job of reaching out to others for advice, guidance, and mentoring. Finally, I wanted to portray principals not as infallible superheroes or distant bureaucrats but rather as real people toiling in the place where theory meets reality, priorities are sorted, balance is sought, and both mistakes and differences are made.

This story of Principal Joe Gentry's first semester is a mix of experience, imagination, and plausibility. It portrays his initial experiences with the pursuit of the elusive practice called *school leadership*. I invite readers to apply school leadership standards and evaluate the skill, wisdom, and judgment he and his two friends (also new principals) exercise and to anticipate what happens during the second half of the school year, which is revealed in this book's companion, *Seeking Balance: The Story of a Principal's Second Semester.*

Introduction

Principals are familiar with the pacing of the school year. While some aspects of the job are constant, others are unique and tied to the times at which they occur. As a result, the book's chapters are divided into months to reflect those times and issues. Questions at the end of each chapter are intended as starters. Readers will certainly have others.

The story begins in March, as Joe Gentry and two graduate school friends meet to discuss the next steps in their careers, and continues through the summer as Joe begins to learn about his new school and community, Pinicon Secondary School. In August, teachers and students arrive and the new Principal Gentry is immersed in his new role. As autumn rolls into winter, he works to communicate his philosophy, understand his new school's culture, find personal and professional balance, and lead.

This first part of the story concludes during winter break, when Principal Gentry and his two friends reunite to reflect on lessons learned in their first semesters. Meeting back at their familiar campus hangout, Joe looks toward his coming midyear evaluation. Together, he and his friends vow to combine those lessons with their goals for the second semester. As noted, that part of the story is revealed in this book's companion, *Seeking Balance: The Story of a Principal's Second Semester.*

Chapter One

March

Looking to Lead

THE DEBRIEF

Mark Sutton's beat-up Chevy Blazer careened into the parking lot of the Northgate Grill, leftover sand from winter scratching beneath his worn tires. As usual, he was late. That's the way the stocky, former high school linebacker lived—a little rushed and haphazard. Known to most as "Sutt," he was often irreverent and loud and embraced his blustery reputation. He was late for a spring break lunch with his grad school classmate and fellow wannabe principal, Kristi Peters.

Kristi, in many ways, was Sutt's polar opposite. Where Sutt was boisterous and a little uncouth, Kristi was serious and cerebral. Tidy. She preferred marathons and poetry to Sutt's love of hunting and football. Sutt refused to use the term *industrial technology* for the courses he taught. "I'm a freaking shop teacher. Call it what it is," he'd say. Kristi was a self-described "special educator." In contrast to Sutt's rusty 4x4, her Toyota Prius was kept in showroom condition. Some admired her organized, alphabetized life. Others found it exhausting and a bit rigid.

Sutt boasted that he had raised himself because his parents had been "too busy drinking and smoking" to worry about him. Kristi had been the quintessential military brat, bouncing around posts across the world with her single father, a career army officer. The parenting she received was as hands-on and structured as Sutt's was absent and laissez-faire.

1

Between Kristi's thoughtful, measured manner and Sutt's bravado was Joe Gentry, the third member of their grad school triumvirate. He was a social studies teacher and basketball coach who might have also been at home in advertising or politics. Joe was more extroverted than Kristi and more tactful than Sutt. In contrast to Sutt's hands-off upbringing and Kristi's world travels, Joe experienced a somewhat idyllic childhood, close to his parents and younger sister and involved in sports and school activities. Joe attended college on a basketball scholarship while Sutt had worked at a host of construction and other jobs to pay for junior college and university tuition. Kristi had attended a highly selective private women's college.

To everyone's surprise and despite their differences, after two years of carpooling to grad school, working on projects, and sorting through countless scenarios posed by their professors, the three formed a friendship that transcended their interest in becoming principals. In many ways, they stood at equidistant points on a style continuum, with Sutt and his never-ending bluster and self-deprecating humor on one end, Joe's diplomacy and wit in the middle, and Kristi's introspective and ponderous manner on the other end. Their styles and backgrounds complemented one another and, despite their differences, the three enjoyed a mutual, though unexpected, respect.

The months since graduation had passed quickly and, despite their best intentions, they had only been able to chat a few times on the phone and online. The three had grown so comfortable with each other that not meeting once a week for classes and often on weekends to collaborate felt awkward. They missed seeing each other and had arranged a meeting to catch up.

After setting the date, Professor Darrell Summers had asked Joe to come by his office the same afternoon. That Joe was a favorite student had been obvious to some in their cohort of wannabe principals and they had teased him mercilessly for it. Now that the venerable professor who was nearing retirement from Central State University had summoned Joe to his office a few months after graduation, the evidence was indisputable, Sutt said. Joe planned to join them as soon as he was finished with meeting with Professor Summers.

Kristi was squeezing lemon juice onto her salad when Sutt strode to the table.

"Hit me up with that tenderloin, Larry," he hollered to the cook in the familiar campus hangout. "Sorry I'm late, but we've been down that road."

"We have, at that. How've you been?"

"Good, good," Sutt said, grasping for the remote control and turning the channel to ESPN. "Should we kick that pretty boy Joe out of our group since we now have proof that he's Summers's favorite? Maybe he'll big-time us and not even show today. Dude's probably gonna start going to art museums with Summers now."

"Very possible," Kristi agreed jokingly.

They compared notes on open principal positions they'd seen advertised. Sutt said he had submitted a dozen or so applications, mostly for assistant principal positions in high schools of about a thousand students. He said he was looking for the "right one," but also said the right one would be one that allowed him to start paying back his student loans.

"I will say I'm looking forward to seeing Oswald and the dump we call Oswald High School in my rearview mirror. The sooner, the better." Oswald had a well-earned reputation as a tough railroad and river city with one of the state's highest unemployment rates and few prospects for improving its fortunes. The economic downturn had not been kind to the shrinking city of sixty thousand.

Kristi also felt ready for her next step professionally. Most of her classmates said she was as ready as anyone, though some wondered if her quiet personality and nonflashy style might make it hard to get noticed. Perhaps it was easier to overlook Kristi in a room full of guys like Sutt, who were always talking and backslapping—the consummate good ol' boy. That was not her forte. A serious focus on instruction and meticulous planning were her bread and butter.

Kristi said she had applied for only one elementary principal position. "I'll probably never get a look, but I sent my materials to Winthrop. I'd love to just get an interview," she said, describing a small district tucked away in the scenic hills of the southeast part of the state. Winthrop had plenty of quaint small-town charm—quite unlike Oswald.

"Yeah. Everyone probably wants that one, but you could do it."

They reflected on their paths toward becoming principals and their experiences in graduate school—how some professors seemed so knowledgeable and wise that students wondered if anything ever fazed them as leaders, while some others seemed hopelessly out of touch. Sutt sometimes wondered whether they'd spent any time in real schools.

"It's so funny how things turn out. We all found our styles. I thought you were all show for the first two weeks," Kristi said, telling Sutt something he already knew.

"Yeah, well, I wouldn't have put you on my social calendar either, sister. But BS aside, I learned a lot, maybe as much from you guys as from the professors," he said, admiring his tenderloin.

ONE TO TAKE A LOOK AT

Professor Darrell Summers's office befitted his buttoned-down image. Situated on the sixth floor of the School of Education building, it overlooked a campus green space that was nearly as manicured as the professor's office. Although all of their classmates admired Professor Summers, some found him intimidating. Those with sufficient reason to visit the professor's office sometimes felt uncomfortable walking down the long hallway that led to "Summers's Lair," as Sutt called it. Joe felt especially privileged to have received the invitation with his impending retirement.

Professor Summers began the conversation inquiring about the funeral of Joe's grandfather, Elton Rash, which had been a couple of weeks prior.

"I'll bet the funeral was a celebration of a good life," said Professor Summers.

"You could say that, I guess," Joe responded, shifting in his chair. "He'd been sick for years and we knew it was coming, but it was harder than we expected. You think you're ready, but it's different when it finally comes. But yeah, some good stories. He liked to say he had a helluva run."

The professor listened intently as Joe shared some stories about the tough old German farmer with a penchant for profanity and a roaring laugh. Summers was a good listener.

"Sounds like quite a guy. I think I would have liked him," he speculated. Joe agreed.

Although Elton Rash and Dr. Darrell Summers were quite different, the professor was right. They would have liked each other. Joe had never seen his grandfather in anything but bib overalls. In contrast, over beers at after-class meetings at the Northgate, Joe and his classmates speculated about whether Professor Summers ever wore anything but meticulously pressed dress pants. Beneath their opposite backgrounds, Joe knew the old farmer and distinguished professor had some things in common—an old-fashioned work ethic, a wry sense of humor, and a love of small-town diners and home-cooked food. And a lot of common sense. Envisioning himself as a new leader, Joe had begun actively thinking about how he could be more like both men.

After updates on Joe's wife and children and his picks for the NCAA basketball tournament, Professor Summers turned things to Joe's future.

"So what's next for you, job wise, Joe?"

"Wish I knew. I'm not sure I'm ready to be a principal."

"That's pretty common. You've had a lot of other things to deal with. Important ones."

"As you know, I tend to overanalyze things."

"There's no question the timing and fit have to be *right*, but it will never be *perfect*. Big difference. There is one job I think you should really take a look at. It's Pinicon Secondary."

The state legislature had recently passed some sweeping changes in education. Chief among these was legislation that brought about greater sharing of everything from administrative duties to curriculum, transportation, teachers, and food service between school districts. The law also allowed students to transfer from one school to another more easily.

"Essentially, adjacent districts will start sharing all sorts of things and the state will encourage it with some money," Summers explained.

Most observers said the legislation was the result of complicated high-level political horse-trading between various, often-competing interests. Urban schools had sought and received greater flexibility in meeting state requirements. Smaller schools gained long-sought access to specialized courses and programs offered at larger schools, while still maintaining their local identities. And the governor and legislature touted their support of education by increasing schools' flexibility and accountability and saving taxpayer dollars at the same time. While no side got everything it wanted, each got enough things on its wish list and the legislation was passed.

Summers explained that the Pinicon and Kessler districts were poised to begin a sharing agreement. Pinicon was a K–12 district enrolling about eight hundred students. Situated in a quaint Main Street small town, it enjoyed a solid reputation as a "good system," though Summers often cautioned that most people's measure of a good school was a winning football team, a neatly trimmed lawn, and a good marching band. Despite a flat budget, Pinicon had maintained a solid enrollment and benefited from its proximity to Kessler, a city of about fifty thousand just ten miles away. Pinicon and Kessler would maintain their own school boards, but share a superintendent, transportation, budget, food service, and so on, with the much larger Kessler Central Office taking the lead. The districts would also share some teachers and programs.

"There are a few reasons you should look at Pinicon. First, Jerry Hughes will pretty much pick the principal as he rides off into retirement. We go way back and I can probably get you an interview. I don't know how much you know about Dr. Carol Zylstra. She'll be the superintendent for both schools and she's *really* good. She understands instruction and has great vision. Focused on students. Plus Pinicon would be a great place to raise kids."

Joe exhaled, wheels turning. He had assumed Professor Summers's invitation represented something beyond a social call. Was this the push that would help him decide he was ready to be a principal? Maybe Professor Summers's oft-repeated mantra that opportunities often come at inopportune times was proving true. Or maybe it was a well-intentioned heads-up from a caring mentor, but not quite the right time for Joe and his family.

Joe had been in Summers's office longer than planned and felt sure Sutt and Kristi were growing impatient at the Northgate, wild with speculation about what was taking so long. He thanked the professor profusely and promised to be in touch if he decided to apply for the job.

THE RIGHT TIME

Claire and Joe Gentry began dating in high school and had survived a lot together. From the ups and downs of high school romance to a long-distance relationship while attending different universities, their longtime friends said they were made for each other. The two had solidified their bond when Claire's parents died in a car accident during her first semester of college. Their relationship was tested and strengthened again through Claire's sooner-than-planned pregnancy with Elliott the next year. Now, fifteen years later, they had grown up together, literally and figuratively. Joe liked to say that Claire was the tough one for shining through the loss of her parents and a surprise pregnancy as a nineteen-year-old college student.

When the professor's invitation came, Claire had suggested the family make it a spring break day trip. She dropped Joe off to meet with Professor Summers while she and the kids, eighth-grade Elliott and four-year-old Margaret, hit the mall. This would give everyone a good day out and still give Joe time to meet with Sutt and Kristi.

Although Claire's background was in interior design and she'd only met Summers once, she could see why Joe and his classmates admired him so much. The widely respected school-administrator-turned-professor had a reputation for high standards and far-reaching connections. It seemed that he had the names and numbers of nearly every school administrator across the state memorized and had personal experience with a lot of them. When Joe introduced Claire to Professor Summers at a cookout for grad students, she immediately liked him. "He really *listens*," she said. "Not a lot of men do that." She also came to appreciate the bond her husband formed with Sutt and Kristi and the amount of time they spent talking about becoming principals.

In Professor Summers's first course, he'd forced Joe and his classmates to identify specific reasons they wanted to become principals. He insisted that a love for kids was a baseline expectation for anyone in "school business" and that there had to be more—some transformative experiences, a desire for greater impact, more money, wanting to start schools over and do it right, something. "When reality calls, you'd better identify your reasons and be honest with yourself about what they are," he warned.

Joe's reasons were multiple. He grew restless easily and was unimpressed with the principals he'd worked for during his twelve-year teaching career. As years wore on he found himself doubting that people grew up *wanting* to be principals, but said, "I know I can do better than some of these guys."

Sutt's reason was more practical. As the father of four, he needed the money. He was proud of his working-class roots but vowed that his children would enjoy more financial and emotional support than he had known as a kid. He thought being a principal could make that happen and provide enough income that his wife, Jen, could stay home with their kids. They wouldn't be rich, but it would be a step up.

Kristi was driven by a sense of mission, particularly for special-needs students. Classmates often found her knowledge of the law, particularly special education, intimidating. She was never the first to speak up, but when she did, her words were always influential. Her answer to Professor Summers's query into their reasons for seeking to become principals was succinct: "Because I want to build a system that stops throwing kids to the curb."

Through graduate school and his internship experiences, Joe found himself speculating on how Professor Summers would handle routine school issues—student discipline and learning, teachers who seemed unwilling or unable to collaborate, parents who were impossible to please. In addition to *what* he thought Summers would do, he found himself drawn to the *way* the professor approached things. Summers possessed an inner calm that, even when describing bizarre or heartbreaking scenarios, Joe found amazing. Like his grandfather, Summers was never rattled.

With the unexpectedly difficult and drawn-out death of his cancer-ravaged grandfather, Elton Rash, behind them, Claire knew the invitation to Summers's office was just what Joe needed. The March breeze held a hint of spring, though any realist knew it was probably still six Midwestern weeks away. She sensed they were ready for the next step in their lives and that Professor Summers was probably introducing Joe to such an opportunity. She knew that Joe's propensity to overanalyze was about to kick in. She picked up a bottle of red wine, aptly labeled "Crunch Time," for the coming discussion with her husband.

She knew it was a decision he needed to make professionally. Claire also knew that Joe would look to her for confirmation—or approval—of what he was thinking. So went the process between the two who'd first begun clicking at age fifteen. She usually knew before he did.

QUESTIONS

1. What are your reasons for pursuing the principalship? How will you know the right time?
2. What type of school appeals to you and why?

Chapter Two

June

Moving On

NEW OPPORTUNITIES

Nobody who knew Kristi Peters was surprised when she was offered the principalship at Winthrop Elementary School, although she had been the only candidate who lacked administrative experience. Perhaps her subtle blend of enthusiasm and calm demeanor had won over the committee. Or perhaps it was her near-encyclopedic knowledge of the latest thinking in educational leadership; Joe and Sutt swore she had a photographic memory. Whatever the reasons for her selection, she had never been more excited than she was the day she accepted the job.

She'd become only the third principal at Winthrop Elementary school in the past twenty-five years. Although the three-section K–5 elementary building had experienced remarkable stability, it was anything but stagnant. Much of the professional learning initiatives under way in other nearby schools had developed at Winthrop Elementary. Skilled grant writing had provided teachers with a wealth of equipment and professional growth opportunities, including an exchange program with elementary teachers in Taiwan. As a result, teacher turnover in the building was rare. Many suspected that Kristi didn't fully realize what an accomplishment it had been for her to land the job.

Sutt said he was tired of "being a freaking bridesmaid," finishing second (or lower) for several assistant high school principal positions. In his sarcastic way, he blamed his failure to find a principalship on everything from the condition of his truck to being a thirty-five-year-old white guy to schools not wanting "a redneck shop teacher" for a principal.

Sutt had resigned himself to another year of making toolboxes when some unexpected things happened at Oswald High School (OHS). The veteran principal was coached into retirement by an increasingly frustrated superintendent and board and replaced by Rudy Carlson, a former college football player with a reputation as a charismatic, no-nonsense leader. He would be Oswald's first African American school administrator, which raised some eyebrows in town.

The change in leadership bothered some of Oswald's old guard, who resented that the principal had been forced out. Others insisted that OHS had suffered from years of neglect and a lack of direction. Sutt welcomed the change and said the lack of direction and malaise that permeated OHS was what made him want to leave.

One spring evening, Sutt was working late in the shop when he answered his cell phone to hear Rudy Carlson's voice. He said the search for an assistant principal had been reopened because the initial choice had reneged on her commitment after her husband visited Oswald. *No surprise there*, Sutt thought.

Rudy knocked him off balance when he said, "I know we just met for a few minutes when I was in town and that you've been wanting to leave Oswald . . ." *How did he know that?* ". . . but I want you to think about the assistant principal spot. I need someone who knows where the bodies are buried, if you know what I mean. And I need to know quickly, because things are moving fast."

Sutt stammered that he could apply for the job if Rudy wanted him to.

"I'm not talking about you *applying*. I'm asking if you want *the job*."

Sutt paused, caught flat-footed. "If you put it that way, sure."

"All right. Expect a call from HR. They have some paperwork. I'll be in touch."

It felt like a movie. One minute Sutt had been pirating parts from a broken-down machine to repair another. The next, he seemed to have been installed as assistant principal. He didn't even know what kind of salary to expect. Maybe no one else wanted the job. He had more questions than answers, but that was usually the way things went in Sutt's life.

Despite the number of times they had heard Sutt say how much he wanted to "get the hell out of Oswald," Joe and Kristi felt the job was a great fit. Sutt certainly knew where the bodies were buried and how things had been let slide. Some Internet snooping led all three to conclude that Rudy Carlson was coming in on a turnaround mission, or what Professor Summers liked to call the "New Sheriff Plan."

Sutt still wondered how down-and-out Oswald attracted the charismatic Rudy Carlson. He worried that Carlson might be long on charisma but short on everything else. Why come to Oswald High School, of all places? Couldn't he find someplace better? Questions aside, he told Joe and Kristi that he couldn't wait to get started. "Plus, I can't get a job anywhere else." He joked that his beat-up Chevy Blazer couldn't survive a move and that he'd go back to making toolboxes if things didn't work out.

Joe's opportunity came as the 7–12 principal at Pinicon Secondary School. Although he was careful to not see his new job through entirely rose-colored glasses, Professor Summers's description seemed accurate. Joe had been impressed throughout the interview process, just as Summers predicted.

The three gathered under a clear-blue sky on the Northgate's patio for what they knew would be the last face-to-face meeting for a while. All three were busy managing different phases of their personal and professional transitions. Sutt complained that he needed an advance on his new salary so he could "buy some principal clothes." Kristi, unattached and mobile, had already begun transitioning into a new apartment in Winthrop with near-military precision. Joe and Claire had not yet sold their current house and found the prospect of two mortgages daunting, but crossed their fingers and bought a house in Pinicon with the help of Gene DeVore, a Pinicon School Board member and local banker. It was all pretty new.

"My God, man, what kind of jack are they paying you?" Sutt asked. "Must be a ton if you're buying a place in Pinicon and keeping the other one as a vacation home."

"Funny. There wasn't much to choose from in Pinicon and we've gotta live there," Joe explained, applying Professor Summers's advice that people typically expect the principal to live in the community.

Sipping her lemonade, Kristi spoke. "I'm going to ask a Summers question here. In a few words, what's the mission at each of our schools?"

Sutt spoke first. "Rudy Carlson is clearly on the New Sheriff Plan, but not just kicking the kids back in line. The superintendent and board want better teaching, test scores, and all that, but Rudy talks a lot about the *student experience*. He knows things were let slide for too long." Sutt was clearly looking forward to the challenge. And the irony of his opportunity—and excitement—coming at Oswald High School was lost on no one.

Sutt nodded in Joe's direction. "I feel like mine's a cross between making sure Pinicon stays Pinicon, but getting benefits out of sharing with Kessler. I'm a little nervous about that and the old superintendent being gone. With him not around, I worry that people will feel like they got taken over by Kessler. And they have a rookie principal who might be in over his head."

Kristi listened intently and asked, "But didn't Summers say the superintendent stayed too long?" Like Summers, she was a good listener.

"He did say that, yeah."

After a little more discussion of Pinicon, Kristi said she was still surprised she got the job. "The mission for me is probably to be taken seriously as a leader."

"Seems like they took you pretty seriously when they picked you instead of the experienced applicants," Joe said.

"No shit," Sutt agreed.

All three had starting dates of July 1 looming. The elephant in the room was the excitement for their new endeavors coupled with a tinge of sadness that time together would be hard to come by, given the distance between their new homes.

Sutt nodded slightly. "I think classes and our internships have done a lot to get us ready, but I'm pretty sure we're gonna have to learn a lot more in the next few months. Like Summers said, reality is gonna be calling. Let's set up monthly chats on Skype to check on each other. Face it, you guys are gonna need my help!" His bravado was constant.

After more teasing about who would need the most help, they agreed to make an effort to stay in close, regular contact.

"Well said," Joe agreed. "And a great idea. We're gonna need each other. Good luck," he said as they raised their glasses for a toast.

(NOT) CATCHING THEIR BREATH

On moving day, Joe wondered who had arranged for a dozen or so Pinicon High School students to help unload the truck. Before he and Claire knew what was happening, board member and banker Gene DeVore had pulled up and was coordinating a crew of high school students and adults, who began unloading furniture. A couple of middle school girls and a neighbor woman began talking with Claire and playing with Margaret in the yard. Joe wondered if he should be introducing himself and shaking hands rather than slugging boxes and furniture, but things were coming off the truck so quickly, he decided introductions would have to wait. The Norman Rockwellian scene felt surreal, like something from a bygone era—neighbors, kids, and teachers, whoever they were, showing up to help the new principal and his family unload. *Who did that in this day and age? Granddad Elton Rash and Professor Summers would have loved it.*

As it happened, the Gentrys had moved in at the start of Pinicon Days, the town's annual celebration. Joe assumed Claire would want to get the house in order as quickly as possible and was surprised when she suggested unpacking later. "We've got plenty of time for this stuff. Plus, the kids want to have a look around," Claire said.

Pinicon's Main Street was full of craft booths, food vendors, and a few rickety carnival rides and inflatable kids' games that the prattling Margaret found irresistible. Joe recognized a few people he'd met in his interview and at track meets he had attended the previous spring and felt the polite but curious gaze of others. Everyone seemed to piece together who they were. Joe had never been great with names and hoped Claire was catching most of them during introductions, while Elliott stood by quietly.

While Joe and Claire knew four-year-old Margaret's adjustment would not be an issue, they had talked extensively about whether a move would be good for laid-back Elliott, fifteen. Shortly before his cancer took its toll on Elton Rash's faculties, he'd grinned at Joe and Claire and said, "I got a feeling a lot of water's gonna roll off that duck's back," referring to Elliott's easygoing manner. Elliott said he was fine with a move as long as his dad could still get him into the gym to shoot baskets whenever he wanted.

Professor Summers's view on family moves had influenced Joe's thinking. "As long as the kids know you're gonna be a family and take care of each other, you could move to Namibia next month, and things would be fine," he said in class. True to form, Sutt had slid Joe a note that read, *Where the $@#* is Namibia?*

The morning after exploring Pinicon, Claire knew Joe wanted to spend some time at school. The big things had made it to the proper rooms. Although she hoped to eventually find an interior-design-related job, Claire relished the chance to get her family settled and monitor the kids' adjustment to Pinicon. Several mothers from the night before had already suggested a play date for their kids who were Margaret's age. While Claire unpacked, Joe took off for school to spend some time in his office, with Elliott in tow to shoot hoops in the gym.

ENTRY PLANNING

He spent a good part of the morning walking the building and testing the color-coded keys he'd been given by former superintendent Jerry Hughes and getting a feel for the quickest routes through the 1960s building. The building was tidy, not fancy, but in excellent condition. Predictably, the key labeled "Master" failed to open all the doors. How would he manage all these keys?

Once he'd been down every hallway and peeked inside every door he could open, Joe headed outside. One of the first things he had noticed during his interview was that the brick marquee sign on the front lawn was blank. As a teacher and coach, he'd always put a premium on symbols and signs. He had usually followed teachers and coaches who had been unsuccessful, disliked, or both, and therefore felt it important to signal that things would be different with him, even if it meant only a fresh coat of paint in the classroom or locker room (which he usually did himself), updated bulletin boards, or new team uniforms (if the budget allowed). These things communicated powerfully and he was into symbolism. Bolman and Deal's (2008) *Reframing Organizations* had been one of his favorite books assigned by Professor Summers.

He knew his job at Pinicon would be different. Unlike his teaching and coaching assignments, here he was not replacing *failed* teachers or coaches. Quite the contrary. He was stepping into a principalship in a school that would, for the first time in thirty-some years, not have Jerry Hughes roaming the campus. New energy was part of his mission at Pinicon, but too much new might be a problem.

This mission felt like a blend of old and new—to respect and honor the pride and tradition that had earned Pinicon its strong reputation, while moving into the future and building upon it. He had to establish personal credibility in the wake of Jerry Hughes without trying to *be* Jerry Hughes. He also had to make sure the sharing arrangement with Kessler felt beneficial to some Pinicon residents who feared that Hughes and the sharing agreement had "given away the farm." Professor Summers loved to rant about how politicians "soaked up airtime on the news talking about the importance of education" while the real work would be slogged through by people like Hughes, and now Joe.

He made a mental note to call Dr. Carol Zylstra, who would serve as superintendent for both schools. He had only met her briefly during his interview and exchanged a few emails since accepting the job. Back in his office, Joe plopped into his chair, which was much more comfortable than the indestructible relic in his former classroom. It was time to think seriously about the entry plan Professor Summers had required them to complete in class.

Professor Summers's entry-plan template was organized around three categories—people, places, and things. Though Joe and his classmates had completed the exercise previously, it was real now. In the "people" category, the professor challenged students to identify the most important people a new principal should meet. Joe included teachers, support staff, and as many parents as possible. He started revising a letter he had written in class, inviting teachers to come in and talk with the new principal, wondering who else should receive an invitation.

Places. He was gaining familiarity with the building and Pinicon community and had seen ball fields, the bus garage, and rooms for which he had a key, but what else? He was glad the building had been designed to serve many more students than it did currently. Perhaps he could come up with a way to utilize some extra space. He knew there were also places he needed to become more familiar with in Kessler, such as the district office, but what else?

Things. Joe's least favorite—policies, class schedules, supervision assignments, curriculum, details. It wasn't that he didn't like policies and procedures—he knew he'd sink without knowing them thoroughly—but these things held less appeal than exploring and meeting people. How and where to start getting his head around all the policies, especially since hollering down the hall to a mentor would not be an option?

QUESTIONS

1. Using Professor Summers's simple template of people, places, and things, what should Joe include in his entry plan?
2. Construct a list of the questions you would ask teachers as you got settled.

3. Sutt, Kristi, and Joe each have different missions as principals. What type of mission appeals to you?

4. Joe, Sutt, and Kristi have a tight circle of support. Who makes up a similar circle of support for you?

5. Joe spends a lot of time reflecting on how his grandfather and Professor Summers have influenced him. Who has similarly influenced you?

Chapter Three

July

First Impressions

SKYPE CONFERENCE

"Home visits," said Sutt, describing how he had spent most of his initial weeks on the job. "Rudy's all about connecting with the community. I've done like fifty visits." Sutt described how Principal Rudy Carlson had divided the 1,200 students at Oswald High School among the counselors, deans, lead teachers, and principals. Every household with a high school student received an offer for a home visit. "I've been in some parts of this town that I didn't know existed—nice ones and others where I don't wanna go back. Interesting stuff, man." Rudy had also been on the radio and TV explaining the goals, adding that families could decline the visit or arrange to meet elsewhere. "It's like the guy is running for office."

Sutt said he had visited homes of affluent doctors in the "Pill Hill" neighborhood, quiet cul-de-sacs, and dingy apartments. One visit had been with a nanny poolside because the parents were in Spain. "I didn't think anyone from Oswald went to Spain for vacation, Joey." While most of the visits had gone well, Sutt said a few parents met him with suspicion. Some held the front door open just a crack. "One lady peeked out and told me to get the hell off her property or she'd call the cops. Rudy wants us finished with every house on our list by Labor Day."

Sutt said that virtually everything else on his job description had taken a back seat to the home visits. "Rudy said the rest of the stuff will take care of itself and it's all about us getting out there right now. And I'm good with that. The other stuff bores me."

Joe and Sutt weren't surprised that Kristi had spent a couple of weeks organizing her office. She had also picked up significant extra duties since she had arrived at Winthrop. Due to a sudden resignation, the district had asked Kristi to also serve as the director of the preschool, which was located a couple of blocks from Kristi's building. "The super said I was the logical choice, but I've got the feeling no one is very interested in preschool."

"Are they gonna pay you extra?" Sutt asked.

"Hadn't thought of that," Kristi admitted. "But it shouldn't take a lot of extra time. At least I hope not. They've only got thirty or so kids."

Joe pointed out that this was like adding two sections of students a couple of blocks away.

"Well, that's true. But the preschool staff seems pretty good and I think it runs itself."

Joe said he had been making additions to his entry plan from Professor Summers's class.

"You know Summers isn't going to make you turn that in, right?" Sutt teased.

"Yeah, but some of us are the *principal*, so we don't have someone to tell us what to do," Joe shot back.

Kristi cut through the banter and asked Joe what he hoped to gain from his chats with teachers. Joe said the chats were organized around three questions: (1) What are Pinicon's strengths and how do you know? (2) In what areas does Pinicon need to improve? (3) What are your expectations of me as your principal?

Kristi liked the idea of inviting the teachers to stop by for a conversation and suggested adding custodians and other support staff. Joe liked the idea. "Listening to both of you makes me think I need to put down all these handbooks and get out of my office," she said.

They agreed to check in at least once more before the start of school. As Joe clicked off the call, he remembered guest speakers in classes who had cautioned how it was difficult, if not impossible, to think of everything at the start of the first year. He checked off parts of his people/places/things entry plan every day, still unsure of what he might be missing. Days flew by as he worked through his plan, triple checked the schedule, and paused for occasional visits from those who had accepted his chat invitation.

CHAT RESULTS

By the end the month, he had visited with several teachers. Though a few had not responded to his invitation, most appeared eager to talk. Some seemed to be interviewing him. A few others looked uncomfortable or came prepared with handouts, special requests, or issues. Joe began assembling a list of the teachers he'd met so far and the feelings he got from them.

Frank Young: activities director, shop tchr, high energy, involved in everything, solid

- Hopes: maintain Pinicon tradition, thinks we need leadership

Jeralyn Kramer: counselor, positive, funny, kid centered, knows everyone

- Hopes: sharing with Kessler is real benefit, not just politics

Allison Jesup: rookie English teacher, ball of fire, immature? Great enthusiasm

- Hopes: she's ready

Mark Watters: English, bit aloof and whiny, seems not to trust administration

- Hopes: for "real leadership and transparency" (???)

Martha Mills: math and technology, hard to read, seems over-stressed?

- Hopes: better communication from prin

Larry Den Herder: Science and fb coach, traditional, high expectations

- Hopes: continued excellence and "the Pinicon Way"

Stu Petersen: PE, probably very dull, near retirement, unsure why invited to chat

- Hopes: kids will be held accountable, admin let discipline slide recently

Carole Martinson: special ed, creative, energetic, seems like fun teacher

- Hopes: to "grow professionally"

June Ramsey: special ed/resource: timid but seems sincere. Can she relate to kids?

- Hopes: see kids succeed

Gregg Altman: utility teacher shared w/Kessler . . . driver's ed, health, coach, high energy

- Hopes: strengthen ties to Kessler since he's shared teacher w/them

Rhonda Prior: enthusiastic math tchr, very proud of Pinicon

- Hopes: Pinicon remains strong and great place to teach

Reflecting on his notes, Joe had more questions than answers. He wondered why some teachers had not responded to his invitation. Of course, some might be on vacation, but wouldn't most respond in some way? He felt bad that his initial impressions about some faculty members were negative and wondered if he was being unfair and rushing to judgment. He hoped his impressions didn't constitute Professor Summers's "Principal's Pygmalion Effect," referring to the dangers of preconceived ideas and inaccurate first impressions. He hoped they were "good educational reconnaissance," as another professor called it. He kept the list on his computer out of fear that someone might see it if left sitting around.

Despite his questions, Joe found most of the conversations encouraging. Many teachers lit up when asked to describe the best things about Pinicon. They mentioned things like extraordinary care for kids, a proud tradition, community pride and support, and valuing teachers and education. "The Pinicon Way" slogan came up a lot.

Their responses to questions about areas in which Pinicon needed improvement were less consistent, and many had difficulty answering. Several mentioned things like "not getting swallowed up by Kessler" and "maintaining excellence and identity." Joe interpreted this as predictable apprehension about the sharing arrangement or perhaps a subtle warning to the rookie principal to not change things too much. Or both.

Several spoke of continuing former superintendent Jerry Hughes's thirty-plus years of good work. Other teachers, such as Mark Watters, were far less deferential to Hughes. These teachers gave the impression that teachers felt unappreciated and undervalued. A few described a local pecking order in which some people were treated like "Pinicon Royalty." Others described how some teachers, coaches, or programs were the "tail that wags the dog."

Reviewing teachers' answers to the third question about what they expected from the principal, Professor Summers's voice rang in Joe's head. "Trying to be everything to everyone is a recipe for losing yourself," he warned. Several teachers, such as Stu Petersen and Mark Watters, talked at length about being "hung out to dry" in cases of student discipline. On the other hand, teachers like Allison Jesup and Carole Martinson hoped for vision and that he would challenge them to become better teachers. Veteran science teacher and football coach Larry Den Herder wanted "real leadership, not an office principal."

The challenge was to address all of these in a way that established his credibility as a leader while also heeding Professor Summers's admonition against trying to be all things to all people and taking on too much. Though he was learning more about Pinicon's culture, he felt overwhelmed. He hoped it would be easier after his upcoming meeting with Dr. Carol Zylstra, the Kessler (and now Pinicon) shared superintendent.

IT ALL TAKES TWICE AS LONG

The next three weeks were more of the same—twelve- and fourteen-hour days trying to use time efficiently in order to prepare for the start of school, without knowing exactly how. Sutt, Kristi, and Joe agreed that everything took longer than they anticipated. Each of their situations was different, and there was no automatic recipe to use.

Across the state at Oswald High School, Sutt was adjusting the schedule for the freshman wing due to a mold infestation in several classrooms. Three hundred freshmen might have to begin the year in classrooms in the adjacent Presbyterian church and a former auto parts store. He had jumped on the hood of his Blazer a moment too late during a home visit and a stray pit bull sunk its teeth into his leg, resulting in precautionary rabies shots. Because the bite happened during work hours, it had to be handled through the district's mind-numbing work-related injuries process, rather than Sutt's family physician.

Kristi extricated herself from her policy manuals and started trying to meet more people, following Sutt's and Joe's suggestion. When a shipment of backordered playground equipment arrived, she assembled a group of community volunteers to assist with installation on one of the hottest days of the summer. She found the group's disorganization frustrating, but resisted her desire to impose order and specific job responsibilities to the group. "Lead from behind and just make friends," she told herself. She laughed it off when one father told her that she "worked pretty hard for a girl."

Joe felt himself gaining ground slowly. More teachers and staff were trickling in, and he expanded chat invitations to include associates, bus drivers, cooks, and custodians. When a gruff bus driver asked if he was being paid to "come into town for this," Joe said he couldn't pay him but that Claire's brownies were worth the trip. The driver stayed ninety minutes. Joe remembered Professor Summers saying that "the cooks, custodians, and secretaries in every district think they're underpaid and underappreciated. And they're right, so get them on your side."

He also tested Professor Summers's theory that a lot could be learned about teachers (or leaders) by looking around their classrooms and offices. He called it "reading the room." Activities director Frank Young's office and shop classroom were a bit disheveled, with everything from contracts for volleyball referees to parts from an old radio on his desk. Jeralyn Kramer's counseling office was comfortable, if not a little shabby. A dorm-room-quality couch, college posters, and scores of smiling students' pictures adorned the paneled walls. Larry Den Herder's classroom was a cross between a meticulously organized science classroom and shrine to past football teams. Team photos, newspaper clippings, and framed jerseys covered every inch of wall space. Joe was looking at the faded calligraphy sign on veteran history teacher Pat Patrazzo's lectern that read, "You must have courage to believe the truth," when his phone chirped. Professor Summers was calling.

"It feels odd to not be getting ready for school for the first time in fifty-some years. Thought I better check in." Joe was thrilled to get the call and sat down at a desk.

"Dr. Summers! It's great to hear your voice. Where are you?"

"O'Hare. We're waiting on our flight to Dublin. My wife thought a few weeks over there would keep my mind occupied. How are things?"

Joe had a lot to tell but didn't want to go on too long. He shared his work on the entry plan, chats with teachers and staff, and initial impressions. Summers laughed heartily when Joe said he was busy "reading the rooms."

"That's some fun stuff," the professor said.

"It is, but I hope I'm not biasing myself."

"I doubt it. Those impressions are important. What isn't said is as important as what is."

Joe said Jerry Hughes and the Transition Team appeared to have done a great job in a short amount of time. Virtually all of the transportation and scheduling arrangements to allow sharing between Pinicon and Kessler looked to be set, and Joe had no indication that any late changes were expected.

"You'll find out if the plan is different from reality," Professor Summers said. "The department of ed. will be using lessons from Pinicon and Kessler as more schools begin to share. How much have you done with Kessler and Superintendent Zylstra?"

Joe admitted that, other than a few phone calls to a couple of secretaries, he had not spent much time with Kessler people.

"I'm sure you're swamped, but don't forget that part of the entry plan. If you don't, Pinicon might be seen as a frontier outpost. And you don't want that."

Professor Summers reassured Joe that apprehension was a natural part of launching a principalship. "Remember, there's no manual, but get some face time with Superintendent Zylstra and Tom McHale, the Pinicon Elementary principal. You should initiate contact. And remember your family. That balance can get way out of whack when you're starting out."

Joe tried to steer the conversation to Professor Summers's upcoming trip, but they were cut short. "We're boarding. Gotta go, Joe. I'm excited for you. Next time we talk, you'll be an old pro! Give my best to your family."

Closing the door to Pat Patrazzo's classroom, he felt a mix of emotions. He had lost count of how many times his professors, guest speakers, and classmates had talked about the discipline principals need to stay balanced and in tune with their families and lives outside of school. He could already feel what they were talking about, even through his excitement.

He also felt some guilt, brought about by the realization that his family had been adjusting to life at Pinicon largely on their own. In some ways, it was good that Claire, Margaret, and Elliott had been busy getting settled in their own ways. They were certainly sharing in the excitement of Joe becoming the Pinicon principal, but he wondered if he was too absorbed in that and not attentive enough to his family's adjustments. As he left the building a little after 6 p.m., earlier than any day that week, he vowed to do a better job of being attentive to his family, even with the start of school looming.

For starters, that included an evening trip for ice cream, followed by some playground time with Margaret. Meaningful time with Elliott was harder to come by unless it was rebounding his shots in the gym. Joe and Claire had learned that they had to take it as it came with the fifteen-year-old. As for Claire, dinner out on the weekend was probably the ticket.

QUESTIONS

1. Evaluate the questions Joe asked teachers. Would you suggest any changes?
2. First impressions are important. Do Joe's notes imply that he is passing judgment on teachers or merely recording his initial impressions?
3. Evaluate the way Joe has spent his time thus far in his new position.

Chapter Four

August

Laying a Foundation

THE BOSS

Joe thought immediately of Claire when he entered Dr. Carol Zylstra's office. The Kessler superintendent decorated her space in a clean, contemporary style different from most school administration offices he'd seen. It was neither fancy nor institutional. It matched her sophisticated appearance. *Claire would love both*, he thought. He was relieved that Zylstra had been so enthusiastic when Joe had called asking for a meeting, which went well.

She peppered him with questions, ranging from the ease of his family's move to an update on his kids and his entry plan. She spoke clearly and comfortably, and she seemed genuinely interested in his answers.

"Some of the specifics of the sharing arrangement are up in the air, but we're going to make it work. And I want you to feel a part of the larger team. Jerry Hughes and the Transition Team did great work getting things ready. And it's a good thing, because you've got enough on your plate being new.

"I've asked Tom McHale to serve as your mentor. He's been principal at Pinicon Elementary for fifteen years and is a great administrator. And it may be easier to access him than someone here at Kessler. But feel free to call me directly any time you have questions. I want to be involved. Tell me what you've been doing so far."

As Joe shared the big items from his entry plan, Zylstra took notes and asked if he had specific things he was concerned about. "In other words, I want to know what you're concerned with as principal." The question was spot-on, as Joe had spent some time reflecting on the change he was undertaking. When he had some quiet time, his thoughts often went to lessons he could take from his granddad and Professor Summers.

One thing he could take from each was their propensity to speak up. Elton Rash had never been one to censor his thoughts (or his choice of words), but that was standard for the old farmer. Professor Summers was also direct, but in a polite, professional way. People always knew where the professor stood on things. "We can confront issues without being confrontational," he often told students.

"I want to be sure I'm speaking up and expressing myself honestly and filtering my thoughts as necessary. I know a leader's job is to promote a vision, but I don't want to come on too strong or offend people. I don't want to be careless with my words, but the personality profiling we did in grad school says I could be more direct and less diplomatic at times. I want to respect the good work that's been done at Pinicon, but also be my own person."

Zylstra nodded. "That's good. And I suspect because you're conscious of it, you'll find a balance that works. Tell me about your hours so far. Some new principals try to be a superhero and do everything. And it's not possible. I'm going to be pushing you to maintain some kind of balance in your life—your health, time with your family, and time for yourself. For me, it's hiking, camping, and road trips with my husband on the Harley."

After twenty more minutes, Zylstra ended the meeting by explaining that Associate Superintendent Don Mitchell would be Joe's direct supervisor. "That's not to say that I won't be involved. But Don's been around forever and is the guy you'll deal with for day-to-day things."

"What kind of day-to-day things are you expecting?" Joe asked.

Zylstra laughed. "That's the beauty of it. I don't think we know for sure yet. But it is safe to say that there will be all of the regular stuff like teacher issues, student discipline, budget, you know . . . all the management. I want you to communicate with Don as needed and as though he is the Pinicon superintendent just down the hall. I hoped he could join us, but he's out today."

Joe wished he could have talked to Don Mitchell, since he had only met him briefly during the interview process, but he left the meeting energized by his comfort with Zylstra. *I'm gonna learn a lot from her*, he thought.

SECRETARIAL SUPPORT

From the minute he met her during his interview, Joe thought Carrie Martin, the Pinicon Secondary secretary, looked like someone perfectly cast for the job. Forty-two years old, pleasant and efficient, she made Joe feel at ease. He was relieved to see her coming into the office in early August, even before her official start date.

She poked her head into Joe's office as he was studying student names and pictures in the database. "I'm gonna be in and out for the next few days, so if there is anything I can help you with, let me know. I'm not trying to do your job for you, but I have a start-of-the-year checklist that you may want to look at."

"Would I ever!" Joe smiled. "I'll be more efficient just because you're here. Thanks for the extra time."

Carrie's list included everything from the forms students and parents would fill out to cross-checking class lists, student and teacher schedules, supervision assignments, and teacher supplies. Joe felt pleased that he had already checked some of the items listed.

"I am interested to know how many Kessler kids are transferring here," Joe said.

Carrie quickly produced a file folder with thirty-seven students. "I sorted them by grade and gender and have highlighted the ones who are out for an activity or who say they want to be." Several indicated an interest in sports, particularly football. Seventeen of the thirty-seven Kessler students who indicated they were opting to come identified themselves as minorities.

She is efficient, Joe thought. "I'm wondering about how to help them get accustomed to things here."

While Pinicon students' desire to take advantage of advanced course offerings at Kessler made sense, Joe was less sure why Kessler students would want to come to Pinicon. He wondered if the "freedom of school choice" that legislators had touted was actually going to happen. *What student would want to leave the larger, more diverse Kessler and travel ten miles to the comparatively sleepy Pinicon?*

Sutt and several of Joe's friends said some would transfer to Pinicon simply for the chance to play football for Coach Larry Den Herder and a greater opportunity to participate in activities. Although the legislation was officially aimed at school choice and stronger academics, many predicted that the athletic tail would wag the academic dog.

"I'd like to set up a meeting up there and introduce myself and welcome them to Pinicon."

"That will be nice," Carrie smiled. "It can be hard to be the new kid. Let me know if you want to spend some time looking at the normal start-of-the-year stuff with me."

"How about after lunch?" Joe asked.

"You got it," Carrie said, launching Internet radio on her computer.

Joe retreated into his office with the Kessler students' files, hoping they would shed light on their reasons for leaving Kessler and wary of the principal's Pygmalion effect. Some appeared to have struggled at Kessler, but others failed to stand out. He remembered some professors predicting that troubled Kessler kids might run to Pinicon to escape their problems or make a new start. Whatever their reasons, he hoped people at Pinicon would welcome them.

One of the forms collected on each student listed their reasons for wanting to transfer. As Joe expected, they ranged from "wanting a smaller school atmosphere" to "more chances to participate" and "a new start." He viewed the one marked only with "sports" with trepidation. A couple of others were blank. Several high school boys listed football as an activity.

A quick call to activities director Frank Young confirmed that several Kessler transfers had indeed been practicing with Coach Den Herder's football squad, but others did not have their physical forms turned in. "Larry won't let them close to the field without those," he said.

"They haven't gotten around to turning them in or can they not afford it?" Joe asked.

"Beats me."

"I've been looking at the files and wonder if some can afford it. I wonder if the medical clinic or booster club would cover the cost of a few physicals," Joe said.

"Well, that's an idea. Never had that before. Want me to check?"

"Let me do it. I need to meet people anyway."

He asked Carrie to call Kessler High School to arrange a meeting space for Thursday evening. "When you have it set, please contact the families and tell them I will be there to meet with them and answer questions. Or try to." He spent the next few hours studying students' pictures and files and transferring key points about each new student into the database. He wanted to be able to call as many as possible by name when he met them. He soon had an outline of his main points, could recognize several students' pictures, and knew a few parents' names. It felt good to be preparing for real, live students.

He sent a quick email to Jeralyn Kramer: *I'm not trying to do your job— and maybe we already do this—but can we pair every new kid with a Pinicon Pal? I'd like them to have someone assigned to help them find their way around so they don't feel like complete foreigners.*

PINICON WELCOME MAT

Carrie said the Kessler High School cafeteria would be ready for him at 7:00 Thursday night, but Joe became concerned when he found the exterior doors locked at 6:15 p.m. A pleasant but confused custodian let him in, saying he knew nothing about a meeting in the cafeteria. All the tables were pushed to one side of the room behind yellow tape and handwritten signs reading "fresh wax—stay off." When Joe explained that a couple dozen families might be coming, the custodian grumbled, "They don't tell us nothing around here, but I reckon you can use the band room."

Joe quickly hung some signs and propped the door open with a chair. He ventured out to the front sidewalk to direct people to the band room. By 7:05 he had a room full of families from all walks of life that was considerably larger than he had anticipated. They came to a hush as he stepped to the front of the room.

"Thanks a lot for coming tonight. I'm Joe Gentry, principal at Pinicon. I know everyone's busy this time of year and I appreciate you being here. I'd like to tell you a little about Pinicon and how happy we are to have your son or daughter becoming a part of our school," he began, passing out a box of blue and gold Pinicon pens. "I'd like to give you a more glamorous gift, but this is the best I've got."

Many of the parents and some students smiled warmly. Other students averted their eyes, too cool to appear interested. Joe touched on his background and said that he was also new to Pinicon. "So, we'll be learning things together." He explained that each new student would be paired with a Pinicon Pal to help them get comfortable. He shared a few facts mixed with bits of trivia he'd pulled from a yearbook. Some things he intended to be funny fell flat, but it seemed the parents appreciated the effort.

After about ten minutes, he offered to answer questions. "I may not know all the answers, but we'll get them or make them up," he said to a few laughs.

He hoped he was not coming across as too informal or un-principalish. For the most part, he felt the era of the stodgy, intimidating principal had passed. But he remembered the argument from the book *Reframing Organizations* that people are thrown off balance when things appear different than expected. He reminded himself that he was merely doing things his way, as he had discussed with Dr. Zylstra. That meant he would be different from the principals he and Sutt often mocked, like Edward R. Rooney in the movie *Ferris Bueller's Day Off.*

After several minutes of questions related to transportation, start times, school fees, and so on, Joe thanked the group for coming and said he looked forward to seeing them at Pinicon and offered to stay around to answer individual questions. Most of the group filed out. The few remaining families gathered around Joe.

"My son wants to come to Pinicon but we haven't filled out any papers," said one father. "Mine too," announced a couple of others. Yolanda Cooper, an African American woman, complained, "We didn't even know we could leave Kessler! We get no information here! Can he still come?" This caught Joe off guard, as he knew nothing about specific deadlines, timing of the transfer arrangements, or how the whole process had been communicated.

"I don't know how the process worked here last spring, but I believe the paperwork had to be started last May," Joe said. "This is all brand new and we'll be working on making things more smooth next year," he assured the group. Yolanda Cooper rolled her eyes and said that wouldn't help her son, who was a senior.

A man who reminded Joe of an older Denzel Washington stopped him on his way to the car. He introduced himself as Jerome Hayes, the father of Javaris Hayes, who would be attending Pinicon. "I surely appreciate you coming up. I want to give you a little background on my son."

"Great," said Joe. "Do you want to talk now or make an appointment to get together?"

"I'm actually headed out of town in the morning. Do you have five minutes?"

"Absolutely."

Jerome explained that his job as an administrator in the Methodist Church required a lot of travel. They had moved to Kessler from Atlanta a couple of years earlier. "My son hasn't had an easy time at Kessler, in terms of acceptance. We don't run from problems, but if we had it to do over again, we would have chosen Pinicon anyway."

"We're glad to have Javaris at Pinicon. What's been the trouble at Kessler, if I can ask?"

"Just being accepted. He's a good student and an athlete. He's found it hard to be both. We worked for a long time to get him comfortable as a student. Back in Atlanta, if he did well in school, kids said he was acting white and that was really hard on him. He's done well in school here, but it's still been difficult. But your football coach is a big factor, too. He wants to play football for Coach Den Herder. From what I know, he's a man of integrity. That's what Javaris needs. I'm sure the other kids who are coming have their reasons, but those are ours."

"Well, we're glad he's coming. And Coach Den Herder is a great role model for kids."

"I don't want to say too much, but it was a bit of a challenge to get this worked out," Jerome said. "The Kessler Central Office was not enthusiastic about Javaris leaving, but others had no trouble getting their transfer approved. Anyway, Javaris is looking forward to a new start." They chatted for a few more minutes before Jerome thanked Joe again and urged him to call if he had any concerns. "That goes for *any* of these other African American young people."

Despite not being able to answer some of the questions, Joe felt good driving home, as though he'd made a good first impression. The transfer families seemed excited to be coming to Pinicon. *Will Pinicon return the feeling?* he wondered.

KEY QUESTIONS

Joe found the sheet labeled "Key Questions Every Faculty Must Answer" that he had developed for Professor Summers's class. Remembering how he hated sitting through faculty meetings while his principal shared mind-numbing information he could have read (or ignored), Joe had vowed to use the questions in bimonthly faculty meetings focused on teaching and learning. He hoped teachers would be open to honest conversation about teaching and learning without seeing them as divisive arguments. Even if the meetings generated controversy and debate, at least no one would be sleeping, as he had seen more than once.

He scanned the list of questions and changed some of the wording.

- What is the purpose of school in American society?

- What constitutes good teaching?
- Is there such a thing as "best practice?"
- React: Good teachers help every student work to earn an A.
- Does a crisis in American education exist?
- How do you know the lesson you're about to give is the one students need?
- Is there a difference between assessment *of* learning and assessment *for* learning?
- Does extra credit shift students' focus from learning to point acquisition?
- What is the value and purpose of homework?
- What does it mean to be an educated person?
- What is the role of technology in teaching and learning?

Would the Pinicon staff embrace the questions like his grad school classmates had?

QUESTIONS

1. Evaluate Joe's meeting with Superintendent Zylstra.
2. What would you expect to see on Carrie's start-of-the-year checklist?
3. Evaluate Joe's visit to Kessler.
4. Assess Joe's "Key Questions" and his plans to use them.

Chapter Five

Mid-August

Here Come the Teachers

GUILT BY ASSOCIATION

School was set to start on Monday. Although Joe had a few more things to quadruple check, he spent Saturday at home with Claire, Elliott, and Margaret. He was up early, intent on enjoying the August sun and the chance to do a few things around the house. He was no handyman, but he and Claire had learned a lot from YouTube videos and advice from the hardware store. He was working on the front screen door when a woman in her early fifties parked next to the curb and started up the sidewalk.

She apologized for intruding on a Saturday and introduced herself as Beth Larson. Joe assured her it was no problem and that he was happy to meet her. In rapid-fire speech she explained that her son, Seth, was the seventh- and eighth-grade football coach. Seth was enrolled at the junior college in Kessler with the ultimate goal of becoming a PE teacher and activities director.

Speaking so rapidly that she was hard to understand, she said that the night before Kessler police had issued citations for underage drinking at Seth's apartment. She complained that many of the details of what happened were not in the police report, most notably that his roommates had started the party and that things were out of control when Seth got home, twenty minutes before the police arrived.

"I hope this won't jeopardize his coaching position, because it's his dream and he hasn't done anything wrong. His roommates caused it."

Joe thanked her for letting him know but said the issue should really be taken up with activities director Frank Young. Mrs. Larson rolled her eyes and said her kids and Young had "never really hit it off" and that she was concerned about Seth being treated fairly.

"Mrs. Larson, I'm sure everyone will be fair and want to do what's best and according to policy. I'll let Frank know that he should be expecting to hear from Seth." She left abruptly.

Joe wondered whether he should finish the screen door or let Young know right away. He decided to call him, since his home improvement projects usually took longer than anticipated and he knew if he were in Young's shoes, he'd want to know sooner rather than later.

"Knucklehead," Young sighed. "We'll see if Seth can adjust his social calendar to let us know. I won't be surprised if he comes to you instead of me. The family has no use for me. I don't have anything against them, but Beth doesn't think those kids have ever done anything wrong. You wanna coach junior high football, Joe?"

"I'm pretty sure you don't want that," he laughed.

IMPRESSION MANAGEMENT

The rest of the weekend was uneventful. He spent Sunday afternoon putting the final touches on his opening meeting with the Pinicon teachers. By then he had been through multiple drafts and ideas. Not wanting to go longer than twenty minutes, Joe crafted his message around an assignment from Professor Summers's class and the things he had heard in the chats with teachers and staff. First and foremost, he wanted to let everyone know he was truly honored to be at Pinicon and that he felt it was his job to help create conditions under which they could be successful.

Second, he wanted to give a clear picture of his background and outlook. He based his message around the four concepts he had used as a teacher and coach: respect, responsibility, honesty, and courtesy. He knew the number-one thing teachers wanted from their principal was support. Professors Summers had challenged Joe and his classmates to make this a two-way proposition with teachers.

"Assure them that they'll have your full support for doing their absolute best for student learning. Show them that you will support their efforts to parents, colleagues, the superintendent, and the media, everywhere. In turn, tell them you expect the same from them. When you've made an unpopular decision, tell them you expect to have a meaningful, honest, and professional *conversation* about it, rather than being trashed in the teachers' lounge."

Joe liked the idea but wondered if it might come across as adversarial. *Were teachers automatically entitled to the principal's support, while principals had to earn it from teachers? Was that a requirement of "the big bucks" referenced so often?*

Elementary principal Tom McHale said he was thrilled to be Joe's mentor and offered to serve as a sounding board for any questions he might have. McHale, a bearded marathon runner in his mid-fifties, reminded Joe of Phil Jackson, the former NBA coach, in both appearance and demeanor. McHale liked Joe's outline and agreed with Summers that not enough principals talk about mutual, two-way support from teachers.

"Whether you include those exact words in your opening conversation with them is up to you," McHale offered.

"Would you use it if you were me?" Joe asked.

McHale laughed. "Ha. Trying to pin me down, eh? I'm not you, so I don't know."

"Come on. I thought you were supposed to be my mentor," Joe teased.

"I am. And that means helping you reach your own decisions," he countered with a wink.

Joe had compared opening-day plans with Kristi and Sutt, who said he was glad to play a supporting role to Rudy Carlson's opening remarks and would meet separately with his freshman-wing teachers. "Rudy wants a jazz CD playing when the teachers come in. That's my only job."

"Sounds like he gave you something you can handle," Joe said with a laugh.

Kristi's plan included an ice-breaking activity that explored how much the Winthrop faculty knew about each other and the game "two truths and a lie" about the new principal. She had also asked all the teachers to share a sentence about why they taught. Joe envied Kristi's skill in planning and, for a moment, Sutt's lower-pressure supporting role. As he leaned back in his chair, he heard Claire's voice and Margaret's feet pattering toward his office. "Time to come home, Daaaaaad," Margaret said, peering around the corner.

THE FIRST FACULTY MEETING

Carrie had asked if Joe wanted any particular seating arrangements for teachers in the media center. The question seemed obvious, though he hadn't thought about it. "Yeah, could you put them together by department?"

"No problem. Do you want the renegades all in one corner or do you want me to spread them around?" Carrie asked, snickering.

"*Renegades*? We have renegades?" Joe smiled.

"You don't show *all* the cards in the interview, Joe. Now you can see the real us!"

Excitement had kept Joe from sleeping much the night before. The feeling was similar to the anticipation before a big game. He reminded himself that the run up to the game was often more difficult than the contest itself, which he had played a dozen times in his head before stepping on the court. He also knew there is no audience tougher than a room full of teachers.

He got to school about 5:30 a.m. to be sure he would be the first one there. By 9:00 a.m., teachers were gathering in the media center to find their materials as Carrie had arranged them. As they were settling in, he heard a few jokes about the seating and the quick summer. Joe made the rounds, shaking hands with those he'd met previously and introducing himself to those whom he had not. He remembered all of their faces from his study of the website pictures. *I've got this*, he said to himself.

Before he began, Jeralyn Kramer, the veteran counselor, tapped her coffee cup for attention. "Order, order!" she said with a smile. "I know we're all bursting with excitement to be back here," she began to a mix of laughter and groans, "but we'd be remiss if we didn't take the opportunity to officially welcome Mr. Joe Gentry and his wonderful family to Pinicon! We know it is going to be a great year and also a year of change as we do our best to continue to teach kids in the Pinicon Way."

Jeralyn produced a blue and gold Pinicon baseball cap with "Gentry" embroidered on the back. He thanked Jeralyn and the group and said how happy he and Claire were to be in Pinicon. He was glad to see Carrie, head custodian Dave Crawford, and a few bus drivers and cooks standing at the back of the room. He was glad they had accepted his invitation to attend, as he hoped their presence would emphasize their roles as members of the Pinicon team.

Joe worked his way through his presentation and slides. He had practiced being conversational, moving around the room, and not talking at them. He included a bit of background information about himself, his family, and how they came to be at Pinicon. "I tell you this not because I like to talk about myself, but because you need to know where I'm coming from."

After the overview, he moved to the three things he felt were most important to emphasize. "First, I'm a firm believer that there is nothing more important than the interactions between teachers and students around the curriculum. That must guide everything we do. *Learning.* Learning as teachers, students, and principal. I've learned a lot from you already in our informal chats and that only gets me more excited. We're just scratching the surface. I hope we can really learn from each other. There is so much potential to build on the great tradition here.

"Second, I know how important it is for teachers to know where the principal is coming from regarding student discipline. If you send a student out of your classroom, it should be for one of three reasons—because you just need that student to be somewhere else for the time being, because you have exhausted everything in your professional repertoire and don't know what else to do, or third, there is a safety concern." He paused and tried to read the room for reactions. He couldn't tell if they liked it, but they appeared to be attentive.

His mouth was cotton-dry, even after a few sips of water, when he started the next part—what the teachers could expect from him. Since chatting with Sutt, Kristi, and McHale, he had gone back and forth on whether to include support being a two-way street. He wanted to begin with complete honesty and transparency.

"As a teacher and coach, I've had four rules that have served me well. I'm sharing them to let you know what I expect of myself, but also to ask that you help me stick to them. I'll invite you to commit to the same ideas, if you choose. First is *respect*. I will respect all people, our school, and my role. Second, *responsibility*. I embrace my responsibilities as a leader and learner. Third is *honesty*. I will be honest at all times. And fourth is *courtesy*. I will be kind, polite, and fun."

Dry mouth again and the room felt uncomfortably quiet. He knew he'd thrown a lot of information at them, but it paled in comparison to everything that had come at *him* in the last month. Hydrated, he pressed on, nearing the end of his pitch.

"I want to finish today talking about support—*mutual support*. Every teacher wants the principal's support. Know that I will support your best efforts to reach and teach our students. I hope you'll extend the same support to me as I learn. Not *if* but *when* I've made an unpopular decision, I hope we can have a professional conversation about it. We won't always agree, but I'll always be open to discussion. That takes trust, which I'm going to work to build. To that end, I'll be asking you to nominate colleagues for a leadership team to help support our efforts. I'm a true believer in the power of teams."

He closed with something that had come to him only the night before. He wondered if the story might seem too sappy, but Claire told him to go with it. "They need to see the real you," she said. "You have to be honest and lay it out there."

"We buried my grandfather, Elton Rash, last spring," Joe said. "I'm not into stereotypes, but he was a stereotypical tough, old German farmer. Fought in the infantry. Not great in school, but had a gift with plants and animals. Smart, honest, and a good man. Loved to laugh."

Joe continued, now holding a buckeye in his right hand, tossing it gently. "Had a million folksy sayings and taught me a lot about hard work, honesty, and family. He carried a buckeye in his pocket his whole life and he swore it brought him luck. He carried it through the war, losing a farm, losing a child, losing his wife."

Joe shrugged. "Not sure he *had* a lot of luck, but . . . ," he said, surprised that the last words caught in his throat. A few smiles and some polite laughter. "I've started carrying a buckeye to remind me of those values. And I certainly hope it will bring us luck." He paused. "Thanks for the opportunity to work and learn with you. Claire and I are so happy to be here."

Applause. Not thunderous, but polite and lots of smiles. Several teachers he hadn't met hung around to shake his hand. Jeralyn winked at him from across the room as she gathered her supplies. Larry Den Herder, the veteran football coach and science teacher, was among the first to greet him. "Enjoyed it, Joe. That's the kind of thing we've needed around here for a long time. I think I would have liked your granddad," he said, with an extra-firm handshake.

The rest of the day flew past—phone calls, stops in each classroom to say hello, and last-minute scheduling problems with Carrie and Jeralyn. In no time, it was 4:00 p.m. and a few teachers were headed out. Joe was encouraged that most hung around, working in their classrooms, in meetings, and chatting about fall sports teams.

Just before 5:00 p.m., Joe realized he had barely been back to his office since shortly after lunch, which pleased him. He was anxious to compare notes in the Skype session with Sutt and Kristi, but knew it would take a while and it would be hard to make it home by 5:30, as he had promised. Loaded with energy, he could have easily stayed at school well into the evening.

WHAT ABOUT SETH?

Frank Young strode into Joe's office with two Diet Cokes. "You probably want something stronger, but that's later," he said, tossing Joe a bottle.

"Thanks. And yeah, maybe a beer tonight. Anything up?"

"Just the usual start-of-the-year stuff. Liked your message this morning. I heard some good feedback from some teachers."

"Thanks. Glad to have it over with. It's time to get the kids in here."

"Uh-huh," Young agreed. "Then we can get some momentum. Speaking of getting things over with, we need to talk about what you want to do with Seth Larson and the party boys."

Joe had nearly forgotten about Seth and remembered how happy he was not to be serving as *both* principal and activities director. Young outlined his many run-ins with the Larsons over playing time and criticism of coaches. "They're a hard bunch to handle. Their kids are spoiled and they know I support our coaches. Mom and dad don't think the boys have ever gotten a fair shake, but they also know I don't listen to that crap. I wish the little shit had come in here on his own and shown some regret," he said. "But that's not the Larson way. Not that I'm trying to influence you."

"Of course not," Joe said, tongue in cheek. "I can't see how we can tolerate a coach getting busted for underage drinking at his apartment. Let's get him in here and tell him he's gotta go."

"Works for me. I'll let you do most of the talking, if that's all right, Mr. Principal."

Joe's computer chimed, signaling that Sutt and Kristi were ready to talk.

"Is it supposed to do that?" Young asked on his way out of the office.

SKYPE CONFERENCE

Joe began by describing his opening meeting. Sutt and Kristi smiled to hear that Joe incorporated his respect, responsibility, honesty, and courtesy mantra. "Dance with the girl who brung ya', Joey!" Sutt laughed. They were more serious when he said he included the point about support being a two-way endeavor between the principal and teachers. He knew Sutt would appreciate the buckeye story, since he had introduced him to Elton Rash a few years earlier. "That lucky buckeye thing is awesome. I bet they loved it," Sutt howled.

"Larry Den Herder did," Joe related.

"Isn't that the big football coach? If he's happy, you're probably on the right track," Kristi said, transitioning to her opening day with teachers at Winthrop. She had cookies, punch, a few balloons, and her iPod playing everything from Mozart to her workout mix as teachers entered the Winthrop Elementary Library. Each teacher received a jump drive and a few other unexpected supplies Kristi had purchased with some discretionary money.

"They matched my statement about serving all kids to me and did pretty well matching up each others' statements," she said proudly. She felt most teachers had listened with rapt attention as she described her frequent moves as a military brat and passion for special-education students. Kristi's emotions were never far from the surface where kids were concerned.

"I was afraid I was gonna start bawling on day one! I used pics of some special-ed kiddos who have really inspired me and was about to lose it when I see this guy in the back of the room sleeping! A special-ed teacher! Can you believe that?"

"Jesus, Kristi, what'd you do?" Sutt demanded.

"I *could not believe* it, but I was in the zone, so I told the lady sitting next to him to wake him up. She slapped his arm and he looked up at me with this startled look, and I said, 'Dwayne, don't ever send a kid to my office for sleeping in your class.' And then I went on with my stuff."

"That's awesome," Joe barked.

"It just came out. Several teachers told me afterward how rude they thought he was."

"What about the teacher?" Sutt asked.

"Didn't see him the rest of the day."

"You gonna follow up with him?"

"At some point, but honestly I was too busy with other stuff."

"That's one of the best opening-day stories I've heard," Joe said. "I don't know what I would have done. Anything that memorable at Oswald, Sutt?"

Sutt said he had passed Rudy's disc jockey test and that his meeting with the freshman teachers went well, largely because he had known them for several years. It was Rudy Carlson's meeting with the full staff that was more interesting.

Sutt compared Rudy to a charismatic preacher or coach. "He was pacing around the room saying how we have to get to know students *as people* and see school through their eyes. It was awesome. He asked for questions, and this crusty old math teacher says, 'So am I hearing you say that the *kids* are gonna run the building?'"

Kristi gasped. "Okay, then. What happened?"

"It was freaking great, you guys. He stood there and took this long pause, and then a couple of steps forward, and said, 'I'm saying that *teacher*s aren't going to run it. *I am.*' You could hear a pin drop, man. Then people started asking stuff just to break the tension. I'm telling you, Rudy owned that guy. I can't wait to see what happens next."

Joe's phone chirped with a text from Claire, noting it was nearly 6:00 p.m. "I've gotta run, guys. I promised the crew I'd be home by 5:30. Sounds like everyone did great, but I've got one more quick thing." He explained the Seth Larson situation and asked for their opinions. Kristi said he should be fired. Sutt agreed. "Unless he's a good guy."

"Now there's a copout answer," Joe teased. "Talk soon!"

QUESTIONS

1. Are there limits to a principal's accessibility? Evaluate Joe's exchange with Beth Larson.
2. Evaluate Joe's initial meeting with teachers. What do you most want to communicate to teachers in your first meeting?
3. React to Summers's idea about two-way support between teachers and principals.
4. What should Joe and Young do with Seth Larson?
5. Evaluate Kristi's handling of the sleeping teacher.
6. Assess Rudy Carlson's response to the question about students running the building.

Chapter Six

Late August

There's Nothing Like the First Day of School

GETTING THEM ENGAGED

Joe had systematically stopped by band, cheerleading, volleyball, cross-country, and football practices a couple of times already, enjoying the chance to make early connections with students and praise their involvement. He was glad to see that a handful of Kessler transfer students had utilized the free physicals from the Pinicon Medical Clinic. Standing on the edge of the football practice field, it was easy to identify the Kessler students on the football field since they were wearing bright-red helmets.

"We had to borrow some hats from Kessler for the new kids. Don't like having them stick out, though. I'll get them painted this weekend," Coach Den Herder explained.

It was easy to see why Den Herder was so popular. The man radiated an appealing blend of old-school discipline with infectious optimism and energy. Joe fantasized about what it would be like to lead a building of educators with Den Herder's passion. Before Joe could ask, Den Herder said the Kessler transfers were fitting right in.

"A couple of them can really play. Especially Javaris Hayes. Doesn't say a word, just tears it up."

After a pause Joe turned the conversation to Seth Larson, wanting to get a feel for Den Herder's feelings.

"Seth's a good kid but has some growing up to do. These players and coaches know their cardinal rule is not to embarrass the program. You and Frank do whatever you want with him. I've got plenty of guys who want to help me. And some of them act like grownups."

Joe nodded. "I have a hard time putting him out there as a role model for junior high kids after he gets busted for a party at his apartment. I think we have to make that point."

"Amen, Joe. Amen."

CURTAINS

Students' first day of school was now a day away. Joe turned around on the front step of the house, realizing he had forgotten the lucky buckeye. He felt a little odd reaching out for his grandfather's good luck charm knowing he was only starting a new job as principal, not suiting up for battle in a foreign land. But he hoped the buckeye wouldn't discriminate.

At 9:30 a.m., Seth arrived in Joe's office dressed in shorts and a blue and gold Pinicon football T-shirt. Seth complained that police had not understood that his roommates were responsible for the party. Seth was a nice enough kid, but just didn't get it.

"Seth, here's the deal. I'm sorry this is the first time we've met, but I'm sure you preach to the players about things like responsibility. This isn't about the cops or your roommates. It's about your responsibility to serve as a role model. You're *coaching kids*, not working a mall job. Anyone can do football strategy. The kids need life lessons.

"Mr. Young and I have decided that you should be not be coaching junior high football this year."

Seth's voice was shallow. "I understand. I guess that's the way it is." Nothing more. Joe and Young rose and Seth shuffled out. The rest of the day was a blur of phone calls, forms to sign, and last-minute purchase orders for supplies Carrie and head custodian Dave Crawford said they desperately needed. Not one to miss lunch, Joe realized he had done so again.

CLAIRE'S VIEW

Smoke billowing from the grill, Claire motioned for Joe to get off the phone and pay attention to their hamburgers. She was also irritated with him for tending first to his voicemail, then to the meal, and finally to Margaret, who was demanding to be pushed on the swing. Claire snapped her fingers and gestured in Margaret's direction.

During supper, Joe tried to prevent the conversation from being entirely about school, although Claire wanted to hear about Sutt and Kristi. Like most people, she had a soft place in her heart for Sutt, and no one disliked Kristi and her big heart.

Following dinner, Elliott went to the driveway to shoot hoops while Joe, Claire, and Margaret walked to the park, where Claire introduced Joe to a couple of moms she had met a few days before. Leaving the park, Joe said, "I think you know as many people as I do, Claire."

"It's funny. I know in a place this size, everyone knows the principal's family, but you don't know any of them. Most people have been really nice and introduced themselves, but it's like some have never been the new person and don't know how to welcome somebody."

Joe's phone was ringing. Claire's eyes flashed. "Don't you dare."

He let it go. "Sorry. Sutt and I were talking about that principal in the fishbowl thing the other day. He's kind of anonymous in a city like Oswald, but his principal wants them to be a lot more visible. I guess it cuts both ways."

They walked back home as dusk approached. Over the trees of the city park, they could see the glow from the football field lights. In between cars passing and kids enjoying the end of summer, they could faintly hear the whistles of Larry Den Herder and the football coaching staff barking out the virtues of playing football the Pinicon Way. "It feels good here," Claire said softly, her hand in Joe's. "This is a good place for us."

STUDENTS!

Joe arrived at school a little after 6:00 a.m. on Monday, rested. He wore a crisply pressed white dress shirt with a new blue and gold tie Claire had given him. Dave Crawford was high atop a ladder, halfway inside a duct when Joe entered the building. Joe warned him about crawling all the way inside the duct.

"Someone might put the ladder away, and we'll never find you," Joe hollered, shaking Crawford's ladder gently.

Crawford, himself a Pinicon graduate and Ford Mustang fanatic, had the place gleaming. Other than its 1960s-style architecture, the building looked barely used. On his way to the office, Joe dropped a *Car and Driver* magazine featuring the new Mustang on Crawford's table in the boiler room with a note of thanks for his hard work in getting the building ready.

Joe was disappointed to get a call from Zylstra saying she would not be able to attend the morning's opening ceremony and that Associate Superintendent Don Mitchell would come in her place. She and Joe had agreed that it was important for her to be highly visible in Pinicon with the new shared superintendent arrangement.

A couple of days before, Young and Jeralyn had pitched the idea of making a video connection to a former Pinicon coach and soldier who was stationed in the Middle East. They had tested the link three times and assured Joe that the crowd would go wild when they sprang the surprise. "If the link isn't working, we'll just go on and no one will know."

Joe cruised through the building efficiently now and settled into his office by 6:20. He reviewed the comments he wanted to make in the ceremony and pulled up his calendar to look at the week's schedule. He planned to visit each classroom twice that week. Whether he could actually *make it* to all those classrooms remained to be seen.

By a little after 7:00, a few teachers were beginning to arrive and were happy to find his welcome message and one of Claire's apple cinnamon muffins in their mailboxes. The sun shone brightly through the clear windows. "Nothing like the first day," he told teachers.

By 7:30, some students were gathering on the front lawn and in the cafeteria. Joe made his way to the circle drive out front, where parents dropped off students, shaking hands and forcing a few kids into awkward fist bumps and sliding open a few van doors. He then walked to the student parking lot and introduced himself to groups of high school students. Several were shocked when he called them by name.

Many seemed unsure of how to respond to his enthusiasm. Some played what Joe called "high school cool," not showing too much interest, although others seemed to enjoy the welcome. By 8:00 a.m., he was back in the building for rounds and greetings. At 8:05, Carrie called to say Don Mitchell was waiting for him in his office.

MEETING MITCHELL

Kessler Associate Superintendent Don Mitchell was a rotund man in his late fifties. Not flashy, Mitchell wore a blue suit, red tie, and well-worn shoes needing polish. A Kessler School District ID badge hung on a lanyard around his neck. Joe extended his hand to Mitchell, who was looking around at the pictures and personal affects scattered around his office.

"Don, it's good to see you again. Thanks for being here."

"We need ID badges for your kids," he said, holding his lanyard. "Carol's sorry she couldn't make it. You ready to go?"

"I'm ready, and if I'm not, they're here anyway!" Joe laughed.

"Should be interesting," Mitchell said flatly.

Joe wondered if Mitchell seemed dull because of his own giddy excitement or if it was just Mitchell's personality.

"So what is happening this morning?" Mitchell asked.

Joe explained the schedule, including the video link, while Mitchell scrolled through messages on his phone, nodding. Unimpressed, Joe caught himself and thought, *Stop judging.*

The gym bubbled with energy as Pinicon elementary principal Tom McHale helped his students find seats. Lots of new school clothes. Chatter everywhere. Some teachers loomed over their students like secret service agents, while others talked with colleagues and seemed to be oblivious.

Joe introduced Mitchell to a few teachers. Mitchell was pleasant, but a little curt, he thought. On stage, elementary principal Tom McHale was working on the video link.

"Tom, have you met Don Mitchell from Kessler?"

"Oh, I see they sent the B-team down today," McHale said, shaking hands with Mitchell, who showed a bit more energy now.

"Dr. Zylstra's at the opening ceremony for the *varsity*," Mitchell countered.

"So you two know each other," Joe said.

"Thirty-some years' worth," said Mitchell.

"Don got through his first few years of teaching because of my lesson planning." McHale smiled. Mitchell smiled but didn't argue.

BOUNCING JUNEAU

The band had begun to play, providing Joe a break from hosting the underwhelming Mitchell. He thought it a bit odd that the ceremony was mostly led by guidance counselor Jeralyn Kramer, rather than either of the principals, but he didn't mind. He had plenty to think about and this was apparently the way things were done on opening day at Pinicon.

As Jeralyn welcomed the crowd to the packed gym, Joe's mind wandered from the kids he'd met to the surprising number of parents and community members in attendance, to the teachers, to why this Mitchell guy was such a sleeper, to how quickly the start of school had come, and to the buckeye in his pocket.

Each of the fall sport coaches had a few minutes to address the crowd, but Larry Den Herder's reception blew Joe away. The old coach waited thirty seconds for the cheering to stop before speaking. He was direct, energetic, and sharp. *No wonder the kids do anything for this guy*, Joe thought. Gaining his approval at the opening teachers meeting had been a good thing. *Get the opinion leaders on your side and you'll get the rest.*

It was nearly time for the video link. Jeralyn called Becky Marks, the student council president, to the podium. She explained that her father, a former Pinicon wrestling coach, was stationed in the army in the Middle East. In a thin but adequate voice, she told the crowd that her father was engaged in his third deployment, prompting a standing ovation and applause that equaled Den Herder's. As the band and choir situated themselves, she invited the crowd to stand for the presentation of the flag by members of the Army Reserve.

Joe was caught up in Becky's unexpected speaking moxie when Mitchell leaned over to him and growled, "Get that asshole out of here if he's not gonna stand." Scanning the crowd, Joe almost missed Juneau Hall sitting nonchalantly with shoulder-length hair, baggy jeans, and black T-shirt three rows up in the student section.

Before he knew what was happening, Joe walked discreetly behind the platform, off the stage, and down the aisle toward the bleachers. Time inched slowly while his mind raced, asking himself, *What if he won't stand?* He had no answer.

When he reached the bleachers, he could tell the students had been watching him approach and seemed uncomfortable. Joe leaned in, put his right hand beside him, and said, "Juneau, if you don't wanna participate, let's go," trying to be firm but nonconfrontational at the same time.

"What?" Juneau asked, feigning surprise.

Joe repeated himself, more firmly, and Juneau rose and started to walk out, Joe following just as the choir was beginning "America the Beautiful."

On the walk to his office, Juneau asked how Joe knew his name. Joe explained that he'd been studying pictures from the student database.

"I'm not surprised you learned mine. I was in the office a lot last year. Mr. Hughes hated me. Why'd you throw me out?"

"I asked you to come with me because it seemed disrespectful for you not to stand when the flag was coming in," Joe responded. "And we've got some Pinicon people serving halfway across the world that we're gonna honor on the screen."

"I'm not into that flag shi—" Juneau said, catching himself. "What if I didn't come with you?"

Joe ignored the question, mostly because he had no answer. "Watch your language. For the next few assemblies, I want you to come to my office. After a while, if you decide you want to participate in what's going on, you might be able to earn your way back," Joe said.

He shuffled a few papers on his desk and told Juneau to have a seat in the adjacent detention room. As he headed back to the assembly, Carrie grimaced.

FLAT WORLD

Outside the gym, Joe could hear the crowd roar. *The video link must be working*, he thought. Looking in through the same door through which he and Juneau had exited minutes before, he could see everyone's attention focused keenly on the screen, where a soldier stood in front of a rickety desert school.

Becky Marks's father spoke through a crackling video. "Good morning, Pirates! We hope you're having a great start to school," cracked the video, "and we hope you're ready to make the most of it. We'd like to be there with you, but we've made some new friends." The shaky camera widened to reveal a traditionally dressed Middle Eastern man standing holding a Pinicon Pirates flag up to the camera with a wide grin, along with a few other soldiers from the Pinicon area. While he did this, Marks announced him as the teacher of the local school. The gym roared.

The grainy view widened as a couple of dozen children clad in Pinicon Pirate T-shirts ran into the picture, smiling and cheering excitedly, unsure of whether to look at the camera or the laptop that was projecting the image of the packed Pinicon gym.

Joe had goose bumps. Jeralyn was now standing at the podium, beaming. "I've been here for a long time, Steve—I mean, Sergeant," she said. "You and your friends, *our* new friends, have given us the best start to our school year that I can remember. Thank you!"

"Pirate Pride!" Marks beamed, looking over his shoulder at the Afghan kids, who were waving wildly before the link cut out, sending the screen to snow. Joe pulled out his phone and typed a reminder to explore ways Pinicon might establish a long-distance relationship with the school.

Jeralyn, without missing a beat, thanked the Pinicon choir for their performance, the Reservists for carrying the flag, Mitchell for being here, and "most of all the Pinicon students, teachers, and families who make this such a great place to live, work, and learn. Each of our new students has been assigned a Pinicon Pal, but I want everyone to be sure and help our new students have a great start."

Elementary teachers began shepherding their students to buses back to the elementary building, while most of the secondary students lingered. Joe began directing seventh-grade traffic and summoned a few Pinicon Pals to help. As he helped some confused students with their schedules, he noticed Don Mitchell, smiling as he spoke with a reporter.

Joe hurried off with a sophomore who needed help finding her classroom, which led to several other brief conversations with teachers about scheduling conflicts, shortages of desks, and other first-day glitches. Working his way back through the building, he caught Mitchell on his way to his car.

"Too bad you missed the ceremony. That thing with the soldiers was neat."

"What I saw was great. Jeralyn Kramer and Frank Young did it all, not me."

"You had more important things to deal with," Mitchell said. "You can't have a ruckus on the first day. Speaking of which, I need to ask about your recruiting trip to Kessler the other night."

The term *recruiting trip* failed to register with Joe, who squinted at Mitchell. "Oh, you mean the meeting with the parents of the Kessler transfer kids," Joe said. "Yeah, it went well. I think it helped them feel more comfortable."

"Maybe, but it created a problem in Kessler," Mitchell said, explaining that his office had taken several calls from parents wanting to enroll students at Pinicon following Joe's visit. "They think you were up there inviting more kids and that they can just come to Pinicon now. All of that had to be done last spring."

"I met some transfers and parents and tried to answer questions, but it wasn't recruiting. I was welcoming those who *signed up*."

"Well, that might have been your intent, but I've got people who want to come here but can't because they missed the deadline. Cal Murphy, the principal at Kessler High, is pissed off because it stirred up a bunch of parents who are a pain anyway. That kind of stuff has to be communicated through my office so I'm not having to clean up."

"I'm sorry if it was a problem," Joe said, a little confused. He liked Murphy and had worked with him a couple of times on scheduling and ideas for shared professional learning between their schools. As Mitchell drove away, Joe made a quick call to Murphy that bounced directly to voicemail. He asked Murphy to call him as soon as he had a chance.

The rest of the day passed in a flash, but it was fun. The Kessler transfer kids and their Pinicon Pals seemed to be getting on well, all smiles. Most students were finding their way to classes. Several teachers were covering classroom rules, but Joe was excited to see that a few had actually begun teaching. He made it to every classroom to see if teachers needed anything in particular. Most did not. He wondered if it was his imagination or if there was a really good feeling in the building. Joe hoped it was the latter.

SKYPE CONFERENCE

"Six minutes for lunch. But I can down a lot of tater tots in six minutes," Sutt said. Opening day at Oswald High School had gone off without a hitch. Rudy had spent about thirty minutes talking with each class in the auditorium, before handing the podium over to the counselor and administrator who were in charge of their grade and wing of the building.

Rudy had emphasized the new dress code to students. Specifically, he noted that strappy, low-cut, "baby doll blouses" would not be allowed. "He told them he was glad they have confidence and are proud of themselves but that he didn't wanna see that," Sutt said. "By the way, Kristi, what is a baby doll blouse?"

"I think you'll know when you see one."

Rudy had a similar message for the boys. "'No tolerance for profanity and sagging pants.' I'm a little worried about the profanity thing, mostly for myself. He bought six dozen belts and told them he didn't want to see anyone's 'drawers.' We've all got some of the belts in our offices and we're supposed to get 'em wearing them. After that, the day flew—checking on new kids, lockers that didn't work, screwed-up schedules, lost kids. Oh, and we ran out of lunch trays. The secretary had to go to Wal-Mart and clean them out of paper plates. It was a blast."

Kristi's first day with students was similarly energizing.

"Did the sleeping teacher ever come in to see you?" Joe asked.

"As a matter of fact, he did."

"Did you make him cry?" Sutt teased.

"Not exactly. Yesterday, he came into my office and said he had *cooled down* enough to talk with me."

The teacher said he could not remember feeling so professionally humiliated. "I thought he was apologizing, you know, like he was embarrassed about falling asleep. But he was mad at *me* for calling him out. He said I went out of my way to humiliate him in front of his peers. Said he had been at Winthrop far too long to be treated that way by an upstart principal. That's the word he used. *Upstart.*"

"Good God, what did you say?" Joe asked.

"I didn't know what to say. He just kept at it. He wanted to know if that kind of disrespect is what we learned in principal school and all this other crap. I finally asked him if he saw any irony in what he was saying. He said the only irony he could see was me telling people how honored I am to be at Winthrop and then treating him so poorly."

"He must have relatives at OHS." Sutt snickered. "What a jackass. Write him up."

Sutt and Kristi loved Joe's description of the video link. "Winthrop is supposed to be this big technology school. I wish we had done something like that," Kristi said.

"I can't take credit for it. It was all set up by the counselor and the activities director. The crowd loved him, but I missed a lot of the ceremony because I had to take a kid out of the gym."

"Here we go! 8:15 on the first day and Sheriff Joe is kicking somebody's ass. Woohoo!" Sutt crowed.

Joe explained how Don Mitchell had told him to remove Juneau.

"Did the kid make a scene?" Kristi asked.

"No scene, but I didn't know what I was gonna do if he wouldn't go."

"You mean if he was not okay with you violating his constitutional rights?" Sutt asked.

"Oh Sutt, that's right!" Kristi exclaimed. "You can't compel him to stand for the flag. I remember that from school law. What's the case?"

"That would be *Lipp v. Morris*, 1978," Sutt announced.

"Are you kidding me, Sutt? Where did that come from?" Kristi demanded.

"Some of us paid better attention in class than others. You guys know I love that stuff."

Joe confessed that he *remembered* the case and *knew* the school could not compel a student to stand. "It never crossed my mind. I just did what I was told and hoped for the best."

"You win the ACLU award for the first violation of students' rights. That's a riot, but what will Summers say? You won't be his favorite anymore." Sutt laughed.

"Even though you can't legally do it, everyone probably thought it was great," said Kristi.

Joe agreed but was clearly frustrated. Sutt tried to soften the blow.

"He put you in a tough situation, Joe. What were you supposed to do? Tell the associate super you'd like to follow instructions but *Lipp v. Morris* prevents you from doing so? On the first day? No way."

For an hour, the three discussed whether Joe could have handled the situation differently and other sticky legal cases they remembered from class. All hoped for a little more time under their belts before other similar challenges arose, but Sutt couldn't resist one more shot as the conversation ended. "Joe, don't strip search anybody tomorrow, okay?"

COOL CAL

Joe was walking home about 6:45 p.m. when Cal Murphy called. He congratulated Joe on surviving the first day and said that Tom McHale had already told him what a good job Joe was doing. Murphy said the first day was a good one to have finished and that the sooner everyone fell into a routine, the better. Murphy suggested they make time to talk to brainstorm professional learning and other sharing ideas for Kessler and Pinicon teachers.

"Sounds like a good start for you," Murphy offered. "For the first little while, we should probably be paying the district instead of the other way around. You kind of grow into the job. At least that's how it was for me," he reflected. Joe appreciated the perspective that experienced principals like Murphy and McHale could offer.

"I hope our transfer kids do well at Pinicon. I think they will," Murphy said.

"We're pretty homogeneous and I hope it won't be hard to fit in," Joe said. "We've got a Pinicon Pals group assigned to help all the newcomers make their way."

Murphy suspected there were lots of reasons for students wanting to try Pinicon. "The pal thing will help. As for transferring, there are plenty of reasons. A smaller atmosphere, a new start, playing football for Larry Den Herder. Hell, we've tried to hire him a couple of times. And Kessler can be a tough place to fit in."

Joe said he hoped Murphy wasn't irritated by his visit with the Kessler transfer students and families. He was relieved when Murphy said he thought the meeting was a great idea. Murphy also said that the transfer procedures had been very poorly communicated out of Don Mitchell's office the previous spring and that Mitchell was likely irritated that questions were coming up now.

"Joe, I'm not sure how to say this and be professional, but the less contact you have with Don Mitchell, the better off you're going to be. I should stop there."

Joe felt good knowing that Murphy and McHale seemed genuinely ready to help him in any way they could. He would make it a point to cultivate these relationships. While he was not impressed with Mitchell, Joe was glad that Murphy seemed to share his dim assessment. He remembered Professor Summers describing school *administrators* and school *leaders*. "Administrators administer. Leaders *lead*," he said. Perhaps Mitchell was the former.

QUESTIONS

1. Evaluate Joe's handling of the visit with Seth Larson.
2. What kind of things should Joe and his family do to become comfortable in their new community?
3. What impact do you anticipate becoming a principal will have on your family relationships?
4. Should Joe pursue a relationship with the Middle Eastern school?
5. Evaluate Joe's handling of Juneau Hall in the assembly.
6. Was it unprofessional of Kessler High School principal Cal Murphy to share his opinion of Associate Superintendent Mitchell?
7. Is Rudy Carlson's zero tolerance of profanity policy realistic?
8. How should Kristi handle the sleeping teacher?

Chapter Seven

Early September

Baptism by Fire

JOE, WE NEED YOU IN THE SHOP!

At 10;15 a.m., Joe had returned to his office after classroom walkthroughs. He was pleased to see that most classes seemed to be humming along with pleasant, productive climates. Scribbling down some notes from his rounds, his radio squawked.

"Mr. Gentry, we need you in the shop right away," said Frank Young.

"Okay, on my way," Joe responded, suspecting that Young had cobbled together some kind of mock award for having survived the first few days of school.

When he walked into the shop he saw students from Young's Computer-Aided Design class and Merle Richards's Advanced Automotives class standing around their shared office. Bill Kurowski, a stout 6' 5" senior, was slumped in a well-worn recliner.

"What's up?" Joe asked, cheerfully.

"Well, basically, Bill here was run over," Young said.

Joe looked at Young quizzically. This is just about the biggest kid in school. *Who's gonna run over him?* he thought. It took several seconds to process what Young said next.

Young explained that Mr. Richards's class had been moving an old car into the shop, where it would be used for the yearlong class project. Somehow in the process of towing the 1971 Pontiac into the shop, Kurowski

55

wound up on his back with the car passing over him. In an instant, Joe's blood ran cold, and he knew he was not receiving a gag award from Young or anyone else.

"You mean it *passed over* you or did the wheels get you, Bill?" Joe asked, head spinning.

"Well, they kind of ran over me here," Bill said in a monotone voice, gesturing to his thighs. As he spoke, Joe could see the combination of dirt, sweat, and tire tracks on Bill's clothes. Beyond that, he seemed no worse for wear.

Incredulous, Joe looked at Richards and snapped, "Have you called an ambulance?"

"No," Richards answered. "We helped Bill walk in here and wanted to inform you first."

"Frank, call an ambulance. And get the rest of these kids out of here," Joe said.

Young sprang into action while Richards disappeared with his students. Pinicon's part-time nurse, Rose Johnson, arrived and checked Bill's vital signs, and the ambulance arrived quickly. Despite the lack of any outward signs of serious injury, the paramedics thought it best to get Bill to the hospital for a more thorough exam. The nurse called Bill's mother to tell her that her son was on the way to the hospital in Kessler.

As the ambulance pulled away, Joe caught a look at the car that had run over Bill. The massive "old man green" Pontiac loaded with a trunk full of scrap metal and other junk sat near the door of the shop. He wasn't sure which was more amazing—that Bill Kurowski seemed to have no real injuries or that the accident happened in the first place. Joe told Young he needed to follow the ambulance to the hospital. Young tossed Joe the keys to his meticulously restored Camaro. Joe dialed Zylstra's cell phone as he pulled out of the parking lot, relieved that she answered, meaning he didn't have to talk to Don Mitchell.

Zylstra was silent as Joe shared what he knew. He wondered what she was thinking as he explained the situation. He was sure she had seen and heard a lot in her career, but this *had* to be right up there. Joe said the nurse had informed the Kurowskis, whom she described as "country people" who didn't get out much. Thus, Bill's mother said she would wait to hear from the hospital.

"You mean she's not even *going*?" Zylstra asked.

"I guess she doesn't drive; the dad is in the field farming and he doesn't like to drive, even in Kessler," Joe explained.

Zylstra said she wanted Richards suspended immediately with pay until Joe could investigate the accident. "Get a sub in there and him out of the building. Call me as soon as you know something."

Joe hung up, called Carrie, and asked her to have Young, who was listed as the person in charge in the principal's absence, to inform Richards of his suspension and find a sub to cover his classes. As soon as he hung up, his phone rang again. Sutt.

"How's your day, pretty boy? What's up?" Sutt asked.

"On my way to the hospital. Had a kid run over by a car. In the shop."

"Jesus Christ, are you kidding me?" Sutt demanded, unusually serious.

"No shit. He walked away. I don't know how, but it rolled right over him. Un-freaking-believable," Joe said, having a hard time hearing, as the wind whistled through Young's Camaro, which was vintage but lacked air conditioning. They spent the short drive to Kessler Medical Center agreeing that there was no suitable explanation of how it could have happened.

The two reflected on Professor Summers's admonition about special program areas. "Somebody shooting spit wads in the math room is one thing. Poor management in art, shop, and on ball fields means kids get hurt and careers end," Summers warned. If Bill Kurowski had really escaped serious injuries, it would be miraculous. Pulling into the hospital parking lot, Joe told Sutton he had to go, and slid the phone into his pocket, noticing the buckeye. "Here's a good test," he thought. He steered the Camaro into a visitor's parking space and cringed as he scraped the lower-than-anticipated front bumper on the curb. Scrambling inside, the cold hospital air hit him just inside the revolving door. A nurse directed him to the ER examination room.

The doctors told Joe they planned to keep Bill overnight for observation. It was clear that they, too, were amazed that he had not been seriously hurt or killed. Settled in a room, Bill apologized repeatedly for causing so much trouble while he nibbled at his supper. Joe wrote down his cell phone number and asked Bill again if there was anything he needed. Bill insisted that he was fine and that he would actually feel better when Joe left. Joe said someone would be there to take him home in the morning.

Joe drove the Camaro home more slowly than on the way to the hospital. He called the Kurowski house a couple of times but got no answer. Back in Pinicon, he put a few gallons of gas in Young's pride and joy and returned the car before walking a few blocks home. On the walk, he called Zylstra and told her what he knew so far—that Bill had been messing around, fallen down, and the car ran over him. His words sounded surreal, but Zylstra seemed unfazed.

"Thoughts about the teacher?" she asked.

"You mean whether he's any good?"

"Yeah."

"He doesn't inspire a lot of confidence and was white as a ghost this afternoon."

"He's lucky he wasn't seeing *Bill's* ghost. What's in his file?"

"I only glanced at it in July, but there are like twenty years of satisfactory evals. I'll take a closer look tonight, as soon as I get back to school," Joe said.

"I'm not surprised. That's the way it used to be done. Checklists. Write all this stuff down. *Tonight*," she said. "Then, first thing tomorrow, bring every student from Richards's class in one by one and ask them to describe what happened. What were their instructions, who was where, every detail. Get the kids immediately and before they start to embellish or get mixed up. Take thorough notes; keep track of the time and date and all that. Get as many direct quotes as you can. Same with the teacher."

Joe felt awkward, partly uncomfortable that Zylstra felt the need to tell him how to conduct the investigation, but also relieved that she was giving him specific steps.

"Okay. Do you want me to get through all the kids before I talk to Richards or does that matter?" Joe asked.

"Get to the kids right off," Zylstra instructed. "This is a helluva mess for you so soon, but it's important for everyone to see you handling it rather than someone else. It's miserable, but will enhance your credibility."

Sitting on his front step, the last bit of pink fading from the western horizon, his phone chirped again. Surprised his phone had any battery left, he checked the screen. Tom McHale.

"I'd like to help you develop some questions for talking to Merle and those students tomorrow. I have a list, but it would be good for us to develop them together. Merle's awfully sloppy but I can't believe he let this happen. You shouldn't have to deal with something like this, but I guess it could've been worse. Maybe it's that buckeye."

"By God, Tom, maybe it is," Joe said, returning to the front step with a beer from the fridge. They agreed to meet in Joe's office at 6:30 a.m. the following morning.

BURIED

Joe was in his office a half hour before his scheduled meeting with McHale. As he unlocked his office door, he wondered what might be waiting for him from the previous day. He found a couple of office referrals for students and a stack of mail. He had a few dozen emails, some of which he had responded to while he was killing time at the hospital. He dropped into his chair and listened to his voicemail.

The first call was from a reporter at the *Pinicon Herald* who had apparently heard about the accident on the police scanner. The second was from a reporter at the *Kessler Daily Tribune*. Joe hoped that both reporters had found someone else to talk to. Surely talking to the *Tribune* was a job for Zylstra or Mitchell. Joe's third message was from the regional representative from the teachers' association. He wanted to talk to Joe as soon as possible. Joe was glad none of them had his cell number and wondered where he had put the guide for speaking to reporters that he'd received in grad school.

His meeting with McHale went quickly. Joe felt good that most of the questions McHale had developed were similar to his own. He promised to let McHale know how the interviews were going. At 7:45 a.m., Carrie began calling in students who had been in Richards's class. Joe interviewed students until just before 11:00, when Carrie stuck her head in to tell him that Herb Asbury, the regional teachers' representative, was on the phone again. Joe thought he should take the call, lest he be seen as avoiding it.

DIFFUSION

Asbury introduced himself so quickly that Joe would not have caught his name had he not written it down from voicemail. Joe found Asbury's tone immediately irritating and condescending. He wasn't sure what to say, but Asbury seemed bent on posturing and intimidation. Joe explained that he was in the process of piecing together what had happened.

"You're only beginning that process *now*?"

"I was at the hospital all afternoon and evening yesterday," Joe said pointedly.

"Well, Mr. Gentry, you've got a lot on your hands and you're inexperienced. We want to be sure the district is not intending to somehow hold Mr. Richards accountable for the foolish actions of experienced students who clearly know better," Asbury said.

Joe was angry. "I haven't even had a chance to *speak* to Merle Richards yet and I am new at this, but it seems odd that I'm talking to you *first*."

Asbury continued to push. "We'll be happy to help with that conversation, to get a clear and *accurate* picture of things," he said.

Joe had heard enough. "Herb, we're going to get as clear a picture as we can. If Mr. Richards wants your involvement, I'm sure he'll ask for it. Thanks," he said and hung up.

What kind of chicken shit has some legal bully call before I even talk to the teacher? Joe asked himself.

Carrie buzzed in to see if he wanted the cooks to send his lunch up. "No, thanks. I've missed half the day and everyone is probably wondering if I'm here. I'll go to the lunchroom. I need to get out of here and show myself for a few minutes."

Was it his imagination or were people treating him differently? It seemed that teachers grasped the seriousness of what happened, judging from the uncomfortable, almost sympathetic looks they flashed him as he made his rounds. *Try to be business as usual*, he told himself. *Remember Todd Whitaker's* [2004] *advice. I am the filter.*

He hoped he was adequately masking his thoughts, which were consumed by the stories from students in Richards's class. The accounts were remarkably consistent: kids sitting on the Pontiac's hood, trunk, and inside, with others walking alongside it while Richards pulled it up the street with a log chain and his Jeep.

Joe had talked with all of the nineteen students by sixth period when he was scheduled to interview Merle Richards. Mark Watters, president of the Pinicon Teachers Association, said Richards had asked him to sit in on the meeting. Fifteen minutes into the period, Richards appeared.

Richards sat and promptly explained that safety had always been his top priority. "They don't set foot outside the classroom until they have passed the safety test," he said. Joe thought Richards, who looked older than his age because of his particularly slow manner, seemed anxious. McHale had cautioned Joe to keep his anger and incredulity at bay. "You have to step back and take on the role of an unemotional fact finder," McHale had said.

"Am I in trouble?" Richards asked.

Joe found McHale's advice hard to follow, but collected himself with a deep breath. "We had a serious, potentially deadly accident yesterday and it's my job to find out exactly what happened."

Richards began what sounded like a well-rehearsed opening statement in a debate. He described his twenty-plus years in the district and all of his teaching and coaching assignments, from art to history, driver's education, and industrial technology, in glowing terms. "In those years, I'm proud to have given my all to build this program to the point where it is today. Our kids leave very well prepared. And you have my commitment to keep this program at the same high level it's been all these years," he said, with what Joe thought was a hint of swagger.

He wondered if Richards was posturing or if he actually believed what he was saying. As Joe worked through the questions, Richards painted a story that was quite different from the students'. "According to my lesson planning, in order to have this project meet curricular and fundraising goals, I knew we had to begin right away. That's why I advised you that we would be moving the car into the shop yesterday. I wanted you to know what we were doing so you could stop by and see the process or let me know if you had any concerns," Richards explained.

Richards said he had chosen a trustworthy student to steer the Pontiac while he pulled it with his Jeep. The rest of the students were to stand clear.

"Quite a few have earned a reputation for themselves. Jeralyn keeps overloading my classes when they're not successful in others. I'm able to reach them, despite their behavior and the dangerously large class sizes that are forced upon me. Despite the growth they've shown, they're kids and do dumb things. I'm really disappointed in Bill," he said, shaking his head. "I expected better." He slid copies of old emails he had sent Jeralyn and the previous principal, complaining about his class sizes—usually near twenty—being too large.

The remainder of the hour-long conversation followed the same pattern: Joe asking clarifying questions and Richards giving what Joe felt was one responsibility-shirking, well-rehearsed answer after another, with Mark Watters sitting silently. It struck Joe that Margaret, at age four, seemed willing to accept more responsibility for her actions than Richards, who wanted to know what would happen next.

"We have to get a picture of what happened," Joe said. "I'll make a report to Dr. Zylstra soon and she will make a recommendation to the board."

"Students are losing instructional time because I've been placed on leave away from school. If we're going to meet our curricular goals, we have to get started."

"Our goal is to find out what happened yesterday," Joe said, closing his notebook and gesturing the two out of his office. He was sure Richards had never before said the words "curricular goals." He closed his eyes for a few minutes before starting on a summary. After a little coaching over the phone from McHale on how to begin writing the summary, he left a voicemail for Zylstra, outlining what he had learned. Interestingly, Mark Watters had not said a single word during the meeting.

QUESTIONS

1. Evaluate Joe's response to the accident involving Bill Kurowski.
2. Construct a draft list of questions Joe should ask Merle Richards.
3. How comfortable are you speaking to the media? What are your school's policies for media interviews?
4. Evaluate the way Joe handled the conversation with Herb Asbury.

Chapter Eight

Mid-September

Searching for Rhythm

THE STACHE AND THE STASH

The next morning, Joe was about to call Zylstra again when he heard a student mumbling to Carrie in the front office. Then he heard the student flop into a seat in the detention room. He looked around the corner to see Brenton Michaels, a senior, leaning forward in a chair, hands on his knees.

"You here to see me?" Joe asked.

"I dunno. Watters told me to come down here."

"Why did *Mr.* Watters send you down here?" Joe asked, motioning for Brenton to come into his office.

"I dunno. I think his Aunt Flo is here or something," Brenton said.

"Say what?" Joe asked, not immediately catching Brenton's slang implication that Mr. Watters was menstruating.

Brenton snorted. "Nothin'. He's pissed off and I didn't even *do* anything."

Joe read the office referral form that Brenton had filled out. It said Mr. Watters had kicked him out of class "because he hates my jokes." In the section marked how he could avoid problems in the future, he had written, *Not talk to him 'cause he's got no sense of humor.*

Brenton said the class had been talking about how people had changed over the summer. "He asked me if I like his new mustache. I said not really and it probably wasn't real. Joking around. Then he gets all pissed off and says, 'Maybe you're not used to *this* kind of stache, because you're familiar with some *other kind*,' and was laughing and shit . . . I mean, stuff." Brenton continued, "So I'm like no, I get it, and yours is fake. Then he, like, snaps and calls me Brent and he knows not to call me Brent because I hate Brent. And he's like, I grew this stache, maybe you hide your stash. And I said to myself, 'You didn't grow shit.' I mean, he started it, gets all pissed, and *I'm* out," Brenton complained. "It's gonna be a long year in there, man."

"What's your plan to not be here again?" Joe asked.

"Not talk to him," Brenton answered, shaking his head.

Joe told him to focus on the class and keep his mouth shut if he couldn't avoid back-and-forth exchanges with the teacher. "Your language, 'Aunt Flo' and all that, will get you nowhere. You're a senior and know the rules. Act like it. If you're back here, you're gonna make up double the time." Joe motioned for him to sit in the detention room for the rest of the period.

"That's fine, but what about him saying I'm on drugs? It's all fun and games until Watters gets pissed off," Brenton complained.

"You should talk about that with him," Joe said.

"I'm not gonna waste my time talking to him! He'll just get pissed anyway."

"Then you better focus on what you can control, which is your attitude and words. If you do that, problem solved."

Brenton wanted to continue to argue the point, but Joe cut him off and left. Joe was pretty sure Brenton said, "That's fucked," as he closed the door.

OPEN HOUSE AND THE CRAPPY GRAM

Joe loved opportunities to get parents into school and was encouraged that Pinicon Open House had always been popular. The format allowed parents to experience a mini-version of their children's schedules, spending about twelve minutes in each class. The newly established leadership team had encouraged teachers to emphasize the kinds of things students *did in class*, rather than showing textbooks and telling what was "covered." Joe applauded this suggestion, remarking half-seriously that the word *cover* should be banned from educators' lexicon.

Joe tried to meet every family present in the bustling hallways. He tweaked tradition a bit and arranged for the Pinicon Pals to serve as building guides and asked several clubs to sell refreshments. Band director Charity Hampton said she was honored that Joe asked her to set up ensembles at different spots in the building to provide background music. As was apparently tradition, Pat Patrazzo wore his replica Civil War hat. Not wanting to forget, Joe tapped out a text to Patrazzo, thanking him for his enthusiasm. The night flew by and seemed to go well.

Bob and Trina Fisher had arranged to meet with Joe the following afternoon.

"We really enjoyed the open house last night. It was great getting a feel for the schedule, but we were really bothered by something in Mr. Patrazzo's class," Bob said.

Trina took over for her husband. "I thought the antique hat signaled a really fun teacher, but he seemed like he would rather have been anywhere else. In the end, he told us that things are fine if we *don't* hear from him. He said there is another teacher, called her a *young thing*, who likes to give happy grams to the kids for doing a good job."

Joe forced a smile while Trina continued, "He said if we hear from him, it's going to be a *crappy gram* because there are problems."

Joe flashed back to Professor Summers lamenting about how educators often "blacken their own eyes by doing stupid things." This sounded like one of those, Joe thought, assuming the story was accurate.

"I'm sorry that happened and appreciate you letting me know. I need to talk with Mr. Patrazzo, and as soon as I do, I'll get in touch with you. I hope it didn't ruin your impression of the atmosphere we're working for. Communication is vital, whether the news is good or not," Joe said, trying to walk the line between reasonably supporting a teacher and disappointment.

Joe found Patrazzo in his classroom just after eighth period reading a *Field and Stream* magazine. "Wishing for fall weather and hunting season?" Joe asked.

"Wishing for a lot of things."

"I love the hat you wore last night. That's awesome. Something you do every year?"

Patrazzo explained that he used to do Civil War reenactments. "Or what some call the War Between the States or the War of Northern Aggression, depending on your perspective. When I got into reenacting, I bought a lot of stuff and started wearing the hat to open house."

"That's cool. And I'd love to talk about those different perspectives. Have you ever read *Confederates in the Attic*? Great book about those perspectives. Would you ever consider wearing all the reenacting gear?"

"To open house? No way. All that wool is too hot. Not really my style," he said, turning back to his magazine.

"Say, Pat, I had a couple of parents come to see me today about something you said during open house."

"Someone was listening?"

Joe was getting a feel for Patrazzo's one-liners. He retold the crappy gram story and the "young thing" the Fishers had described. "Is that accurate?"

Patrazzo confirmed that it was, adding, "I'm not big on the coddling that passes for parenting now. No news is good news. If there is a problem, I'll tell them. But I rarely have an issue. Probably sent three kids to the office in thirty-two years. If I call home, the kid has truly screwed up and there's a problem. Most people appreciate my honesty. At least that's what they tell me."

"In the interest of honesty, can I share something?"

"The First Amendment guarantees you free speech. You're a social studies guy."

"Right. I love the hat. In fact, at next year's open house, I'd love to see each of us feature an influential person from their subject area. Maybe some would even dress up."

"Good luck with that."

"Yeah. Anyway, I like that the hat is a trademark for you. Shows enthusiasm for history. The problem is that you may have meant the crappy gram thing as something funny or old-school straight talk, but the parents I talked to saw it as evidence of a burned out, sour teacher. And to me, it's less than professional. And a lot of people would say referring to a female teacher as a 'young *thing*' is disrespectful toward women."

"Ah, the principal as the arbiter of professionalism and political correctness gone wild," Patrazzo said, rising to pull the shades on the windows. "That's the reasoning behind the sign. People need *courage to believe the truth* . . . and the truth is rarely politically correct."

"Pat, I'd like it if you chose your words more carefully with parents. I don't like the message the crappy gram comment sends about our school or the demeaning comment toward women. Neither helps us accomplish our mission."

It was two minutes to four o'clock, the end of contract time at Pinicon. Staff often laughed at the way Patrazzo had it timed so he hit the exit door to the parking lot at precisely 4:00 p.m. Patrazzo rose, grabbed his lunch box, and headed for the door. "I appreciate your honesty. Please get the lights when you leave," he said as he walked out.

Joe wondered what had just happened and how and why on earth teachers had chosen Patrazzo as a member of the leadership team.

UNWELCOME?

Although most of the Pinicon Pals were paired with Kessler transfer students, Joe asked Jeralyn to make sure every new student had one. He told Claire making sure new kids got started on the right foot was one of the most important things he would do in the first semester. He scheduled individual and group meetings with the new students and their pals and found the meetings energizing. When his schedule caused him to miss some of the scheduled meetings, he asked Jeralyn to be keep an eye on the program and the kids in it.

When Joe couldn't facilitate the conversations himself, he liked to duck into the room to watch Jeralyn lead the conversations. He admired her ability to make kids comfortable and get them talking. She had a gift and he knew he could learn a lot from her. She had mastered Todd Whitaker's (2004) suggestion that teachers act like they like all the kids.

Joe also knew his ability to get kids to talk was in many ways limited by his job. Their roles were simply different, and he knew many viewed the principal as the hammer and the enforcer. Since arriving, Jeralyn and McHale had both advised him to define the job the way *he* thought it should be defined. Summers had pushed Joe and his classmates in the same way.

"Things are going well, but I have the clear feeling that some of our new kids are feeling a little push back," Jeralyn said, sitting in Joe's office.

"What kind of push back?"

"Mostly about being new. This is the most new kids we've ever had here at any one time. That makes it a bigger deal. Under the surface, I think it's a little more complicated." With prompting, she explained that some established Pinicon students (and presumably their parents) felt that new kids, particularly the Kessler transfers, were getting special treatment and extra attention.

"I guess I can understand that, but I think new kids are probably entitled to some extra attention to get them started on the right foot. It's hard to be new. And if you don't look like everyone else, that's a game changer."

Jeralyn nodded. "No doubt. We've got some differences, but they're among people who've been here a long time. Some of it is Pinicon not being totally ready for newcomers who aren't just like Pinicon kids. If they're brown or tough or special ed or poor, it's harder. And that describes a lot of the new kids."

Joe held her eyes, hoping she would continue. "The kids don't say a lot, but I can feel it. We're going to have to work hard to help keep things positive, that's all. People here have to respect that new families probably like Pinicon for the same reasons everyone else does. Leave it at that, for cryin' out loud."

"So what do you mean when you say it's racial and economic and all that?"

"I mean if all the new kids *looked* like everyone else, it would be no big deal. But since they don't all look like regular Pinicon kids, that's a big deal for some. I've been here long enough to know. It's not outright hostility. It's subtle, but it's there."

"You're probably right. Subtle. So what do we do?" Joe asked.

"Just be aware. We stay on top of the pal group and the new kids but don't forget that it's about everybody. Don't forget the ones who've been here. I think you're doing a great job. Love your positive energy."

Joe asked Jeralyn to keep the climate issues in front of him. "I'm naïve, but think if we handle this right, it might be seen as a good thing. People gotta realize that new families and kids mean the place is not dying. And I want you to be honest with me about how you think I'm handling those things. Direct and honest, okay? I can take it."

"You got it, boss."

THE ROUNDS

He had been stuck in his office longer than he could tolerate and needed to get out. He remembered a veteran principal saying, "When the cat's away, the mice will play; be visible." Joe was nearly on target for the amount of time he wanted to spend in classrooms for the initial days of school but was trying to maintain his focus on visibility, relationships, and climate. It didn't seem fair to let the Richards thing derail everything else in the building. Plus, he needed to see positives.

In the gym, veteran PE teacher Stu Petersen had a group of seventh graders dressed in blue and gold Pinicon gear loudly counting out their pushups. Petersen asked if Joe wanted to stick around for some volleyball. He declined, but assured him he would another time. Larry Den Herder was introducing a forestry unit to the freshman science class and showing a beetle he'd caught that was projected to start destroying the state's ash trees. Helen McCallister's mass communication class had begun developing a list of potential sponsors for Pinicon TV, the student-produced show on local access cable. Rhonda Prior was circulating among teams of eighth-grade algebra students. On his way through the cafeteria, one of the cooks teased about him missing lunch and wondered if he'd disliked the previous day's lunch so much that he wasn't coming back. "You kidding? I'm on a cinnamon roll diet!" he said, to cackles from the kitchen. He felt sure he had scored some points with the cooks when he had tied on an apron and helped serve lunch earlier in the week.

Getting into classrooms, even briefly, was the best part of his day, but sometimes so many people would catch him in the halls that he never made it to his destination. He had been thinking about a good response for when teachers asked, "Joe, have you got a minute?" He'd heard a veteran principal suggest saying, "I'll *take* a minute," but that felt a little standoffish.

Back from his cruise through the building, he smiled when he saw a small paperweight on his desk that read, "God grant me the serenity to accept the things I cannot change, courage to change the things I can, and wisdom to know the difference." Though the design looked a little more feminine than something he would have chosen for himself, he appreciated the gesture, which had Jeralyn's fingerprints all over it. *Timely advice*, he thought. Jeralyn clearly knew how heavily the Richards mess was weighing on him.

He felt good that he'd made regular appearances in every classroom in the building. The next step was to maintain this, while finding some time to be in classrooms for longer periods of time when he could actually get involved with what the students were doing. Ultimately, he hoped to make himself available for some team teaching or at least offer to cover classes while teachers looked in on each other's classrooms. As much as he wanted to do this, he worried about tackling too much at once. *The principal with ten priorities really has none,* he reminded himself.

He waded into a list of internal and external emails, vowing to "delete or delegate" everything that could be handled by someone else or ignored.

Mr. Gentry: I left a phone message with Carrie to have you call me today about my son Juneau My # is 555-893-2700 Ron Hall	Hi Joe—Wondering if I can get in line for the Immersion Grant stuff? We used to take kids to the state forest, but haven't had the money the last few years. I got a note in my mailbox that said to contact the principal for application info. The deadline is Oct. 31, LDH i/d	Mr. Gentry— It looks like I'm about 20 copies short on books for the 20th Century Writers project. Is it ok to order them now? If I go thru Miller's Book World, I can get them quicker but it is a little more per book. I will need a PO #, too. Thanks Helen d
Leadership Thought of the Day: Be great in act, as you have been in thought. —William Shakespeare	Mr. Gentry— X Thanks for your strong leadership to start the year. Kicking Mr. Hall out of the assembly was the right message. It feels better around here already. GREAT WORK! Rhonda Prior	joe, i'm a little worried about some stuff i'm seeing from the Nielsen family again this year. I'll come in tuesday am after the route. ernie bb
Mr. Gentry— I noticed today that quite a few of the seniors were loitering outside the commons area after lunch. They are to STAY in the commons until the 12:37 bell, but I know the bells were not working today. But you might want to get a jump on this early before they form bad habits ☺ Joyce Barry	Hello Mr. Gentry— Thanks for your help in getting the extra desks for my room, but several of the ones Dave brought are older and don't match. Could you ask him to try and get matching ones? It probably just means moving a few from other rooms. THx! Martha 	Mr. Gentry— For the past few years, the sheriff's office has done a workshop with the seniors on leadership. Would like to again, but maybe it should include Kessler, which would mean pulling the seniors out for a half day, probably fairly soon. Let me know what you think. Lt. Martin Beckworth Pinicon Police
Joe— I've got some more background info on a few of my kids who transferred to your place now that you may be interested in. Give me a call. Calvin P. Murphy Principal, Kessler High School	Hi Joey! Can I call you Joey? And can I talk to you about Juneau? Hey, I think we need to talk about some of the Kessler kids and their pals. And let's talk about next year's open house. Jeralyn	Joe— Know you are surely swamped, but just wanted to say hi and wish you the best of luck with the start of the year. Looking forward to hearing all about it. l —Darrell Summers, Ph.D. Central State University

Kessler-Pinicon Administration:

Please see the following link for procurement procedures, logins, PO numbers & routing info for all purchases. Contact me with questions. www.Kess.CS.org/purch. You must use an account before any supplies or services can be charged against your building's budget. Our system only recognizes the new code numbers. Therefore, we will not process purchases that do not have the updated numbers.

Roberta Scanlon
Kessler Schools Purchasing

bb

Joe—
The city says they will be replacing and flushing the hydrants on and around campus Thursday morning and it will discolor the water. I'll put something in the announcements. Do you want to let kids bring water bottles or shall I order some? Thx! Carrie |

Mr. G—Sorry 4 late notice, but just saw the new teachers' conf stuff online. Would luv 2 go if u would write a rec for me? (They are due Friday☹!) Sorry. If it is 2 late, I can forget it. TTYL & Thx |

Allison Jesup, English Instructor, Pinicon Schools

Joe—
We need to talk about the technology funds for this year, as they have to be spent by October 1. There is a committee in place, but I can give you some background on how this works.
BTW, there is a coooool new system I saw that would allow for some awesome sharing b/t Pinicon & Kessler teachers that is not too much $$

TMc

—

Tom McHale
Pinicon Elementary Principal

bb
mtg

1 = immediat
D = delegate
B = backburner

Mr. Gentry: Apparently the city will be doing something with the hydrants on Thursday and the street will be flooded so we can't march. We have practiced the other parts of our performance Friday night, but HAVE to be on the football field (AKA Larry's Yard) Thursday. I don't want a fight (yet) but I know he will not want us out there with a game Friday. What do you want me to do? Charity Hampton, MAE Director, Pinicon Marching Pirates Secretary, NE Band Masters d— AD	Dear Mr. Gentry— My son Davis White is in the 8th grade. We worked with Dalton Myerly's parents quite a bit last year on non-stop harassment he got from some other boys—mostly Sam Shottenkirk, David Burton, and Royce Jennings. Things got better for a while last year but a few new things started this summer at the pool and I don't want them to carry over to school now. Last year was HORRIBLE!!! I would like for you to talk to those three and let them know that you will be watching them. Karen Deluco d -qc	Mr. Gentry— Professor Darrell Summers at Central State Univ. gave me your name as a possible contact for my dissertation research, which involves first year principals. I hope to start my research this fall and would like to talk with you about doing some of the research at Pinicon HS. My number is 555-2274. Thank you. Mariah Foster I
		Joe— Can I talk to you about this sharing schedule? I am seeing some problems with it. Thx Gregg Altman bb- Kessler/Pinicon Instructor mtg
Sir or Madame— We have not received your registration for the mandatory District Sharing Seminar at the State Department of Ed. You are required to attend this workshop. Please RSVP to our office immediately. Ron Fleming Dept. of Education Bureau of Compliance I	Mr. Gentry— Please call me tomorrow morning. I have a question for you. Vickie Goodnell bb- cal Joe— Just realized several of our software site licenses are expired. Not sure renewing them is worth it, but we're using them illegally right now. What do you think? Martha	Mr. Gentry— My son Peter was stabbed in the buttox by Gus Hooper yesterday in Mr. Altman's study hall. It bled clear though his underwear and onto his shorts! I don't know what is going on in there and have tried to call and email Mr. Altman but he has not responded. Has anything been done with Gus?? Laurie McCaskill

Joe— I have again made contact with the campaign offices for both candidates for Congress about the debate we offered to host last spring. They are pushing for Thursday, October 27, which is great except it conflicts with volleyball against Bethel HS. I hate to lose the opportunity, but Kessler can host it if we do not want to. Let me know what to do? Frank Young Pinicon Activities Director	Joe— I have some great stuff that Jeralyn and I picked up on eating disorders that we think should be infused with Altman's health classes, but he says they cover it already. We think we need some help with this, as I know some of our girls are struggling with eating d/o's. Let me know? Rose Johnson, RN	Principal Gentry: Our records indicate that a number of your bus drivers and busses have not been marked as having completed the State Safety Certification Assurance Process (SSCAP). Please go to www.21SSCAP.gov and check your records against what is posted and provide documentation of your district's compliance. Thank you. Howard Fellinger SSCAP Director
	Hi Hon— Have a good day. Margaret is sure missing her dad in the mornings when he leaves so early. ☹ Love you. *I* —C	*del*
Joe— At the Chamber meeting, we were talking about the businesses that would like to be involved in the Careers program but have not been assigned students. Are there really not enough students?? Or do they not know about the program and there are businesses waiting? What can we do? Let me know. Gene DeVore Pinicon Savings Bank	Mr. Gentry— Dr. Mitchell asked me to check on your Quarter 1 Initial Student Progress Reports (Q1ISPR) forms, which were due last week. Can you please send them or direct your secretary to do so? Thank you. Kelly LeMasters *I* Kessler Central Office	Joe— Per our disc the other day about video cameras, I'm attaching this article about a grant program that looks like it would pay for up to a dozen additional cameras at Pinicon if you want to do it . . . deadline is October 15. Also, I'd like to have you accompany me to the regional education day in Jasper City. Think of a couple teachers who should come with us and let me know. Any meal choices? CZ —Carol Zylstra, Ed.D. Superintendent
	Fr: State Rep. Mike Hansen To: Joe Gentry Re: Congressional debate 555-7340	

BLURRY LINES

He heard Carrie talking with someone at the copy machine. "Yes, I think he's getting along pretty well. I give him a few more responsibilities every day," she said, loudly enough for him to hear. "He even had the coffee made when I got here this morning."

Joe took the cue to walk out and join the conversation. "I set attainable goals for myself, like getting the coffee made. I'm all about small victories," he said to Carrie and Mark Watters, who was standing at the copy machine.

"Bet you've had an interesting few days," Watters said with anticipation in his voice.

"There's been a string of them lately."

"Getting to know Brenton Michaels had to be a highlight," Watters said with a smirk.

"Yeah, we spent a little time," Joe said, "which reminds me that I should bring you up to speed on our conversation. I want to be outside when the kids leave. How about I meet you in your room in a few minutes?"

After the student parking lot was clear, Joe made his way to Watters's English classroom.

"I really like the atmosphere in here," he told Watters, referring to the movie and book posters that covered the walls and ceiling. "It has to help get kids excited about literature."

"Thanks. We've done a lot with books that have been turned into movies," Watters explained. "Once I get them past the special effects or having the hots for the latest heartthrob, they really get into it. So what happened to Brenton? You never know which one is going to show up, the bright one or the smart ass."

"Some kids are that way, aren't they?" Joe said, observing more than asking. "He said something similar about you."

Watters looked up from the file drawer he had been sorting through. "He what?"

Joe recounted Brenton's story about the back and forth about Watters's stache and the implied stash of drugs.

"Yeah, I'm sure there's a big one somewhere. His eyes give him away when he's stoned. You'll see." Watters nodded. "We have fun, but they know exactly where the line is and he crossed it. I heard him say, 'Fuck this shit.'"

"When you see those eyes, let me know right away. And of course his version of the quote was a little different."

"I'm sure it was. So I assume we go through the standard deal—detention. He knows that routine, too. Brenton isn't too big on accountability."

"I addressed his language and told him that I didn't expect to see him back in the office, and that he'll do double the time if he's sent out again," Joe explained.

"So he doesn't have to serve *detention*?" Watters asked, irritated.

"Double the time next time, if there is one," Joe said. "Your descriptions are similar. It sounds like the two of you got into a battle of wits. And in my experience, the kids always win those, even if they get some sanction. They know they got under the teacher's skin in front of their peers, which is what they want. That's a nice prize for a kid like Brenton."

"Okay, I'm confused," Watters said, sliding the file drawer shut. "I send a kid to the office for profanity directed at me and you just *talk to him*? No detention, just a ticket out of my class for the day?"

Joe had not expected a disagreeable conversation. "He knows my expectations. I don't know if he's sure of yours or how to respond to the teasing. He'll spend double the time if there is another incident in your class. To me, the key to avoiding that is making the line between teacher and student, and joking and business, more clear. It's blurry to him."

"You *addressed* his language but there is no punishment?"

Joe paused. "He and I talked about it. You and I are talking about it now. He has a very clear picture from me and honestly, Mark, I think the whole stash reference was inappropriate. There's no good ending to a teacher insinuating that a kid uses drugs in front of a bunch of kids. When we go down that road, kids are gonna jump across the line and then what?"

"And then they're *punished*! It's called discipline," Watters said, incredulous. "Past practice here is that students are held accountable for their actions."

"It's important for me to understand those past practices, Mark. We've all got to be accountable. That includes we educators not getting pulled into conversations we shouldn't be having with students. As soon as that started, the bad ending was guaranteed."

Watters's brow furrowed as he shook his head.

"This was my first interaction with Brenton. Like I said in the opening meeting, when a kid gets sent to me, I'm going to handle it in the way I see as appropriate. If it's a pattern, I'll deal with that," Joe said, instantly wishing he had not planted the seed for Brenton to be a frequent flyer to the office. "Let's find some time soon when we can talk about it and understand each other better."

"Uh, yeah. It's gonna take me some time to process what I just heard," Watters said, busying himself again with his files.

"All right, well, thanks for the time and I'll see you around," Joe said, "and let me know when I can spend some time in here."

Walking back into the office, he noticed three seventh graders sitting with wide eyes in the detention room. Carrie told him, "You just missed Dr. Zylstra's call." He was not happy to see more kids in the detention room, but proceeded past them into his office, where he checked his voicemail. Zylstra

said she and Mitchell would be in his office to meet with McHale and him at
7:00 a.m. to discuss the Richards situation.

SKYPE CONFERENCE

Joe was relieved to hear the computer chime, indicating that Sutt and Kristi
were checking in. After explaining that he was meeting with Zylstra and
Mitchell the following morning, he asked what was happening with them.

Sutt said he had gotten approval from Rudy to launch the Freshman
Writing Center in response to teachers' concerns about low writing skills.
The plan had not been all that hard to put together once the freshman leadership team "committed to looking for creative solutions, instead of bashing
the kids and the middle school teachers." Sutt said he was no Ernest Hem-
mingway but that he was looking forward to spending some time with other
volunteers in the center. "I figure it will be a good way for me to stay
connected and show that I'm not just the hammer."

"That sounds like instructional leadership to me," Kristi teased.

"Yeah, and it was way more fun than the oral sex incident on the pep bus
the other night," Sutt groaned.

He said rumors began circulating after a pep bus had returned from an
away football game. "Rudy doesn't like spending time on gossip unless it is
really a distraction, but we've got twelve hundred kids and it was getting out
of control. We had a couple of fights and Twitter was blowing up. Being
back in the shop sounded pretty good when I was interrogating all these
kids," Sutt said.

"Thank God Rudy told me to be sure and have one of the female deans
with me. The boy and girl involved both admitted it. Not the least bit uncomfortable. We asked her what she was thinking and do you know what she told
us? She said, 'I like it and I'm good at it.' I about passed out. Even Rudy was
shocked. It's really sad." Both students were suspended for three days and
the girl would begin counseling, although Sutt said her parents initially objected to the idea.

Kristi described a welcome-back cookout she and her school leadership
team had held a few nights earlier. "Quite a few kids live in a trailer court
outside of town. The leadership team feels like they're always treated as
second class, so we went out there and had a cookout for everybody. It was
pretty cool."

Kristi thought the event had been well publicized, but many attendees were unaware. "We're looking at communication. Notes home, my blog, and things on the cable channel aren't reaching everyone. So we have a new focus on getting messages out in ways that work for everyone, not just our middle-class tech users. I told the teachers it's on us to figure out how to communicate best with our families."

Kristi said her dealings with the construction crew were still awkward, but that they seemed to be getting things finished in a more timely way. She suspected the crew had trouble taking orders from a "short girl." She also asked for advice on a situation in which a parent was demanding that fertilizer treatments on the school lawn be discontinued. The father, a local professor, was convinced that the chemicals used were dangerous to students and could be linked to a number of ailments, in addition to being a waste of money.

"Why is that your issue? Shouldn't that be something for the superintendent or maintenance guy?" asked Sutt.

"I don't think the super wants to deal with it. He says it is a building-level decision. The other day in the parking lot, I got a forty-five-minute lesson from the professor about carcinogens in lawn fertilizer and common household products. Told him I agree with him, more or less. But you guys know I'm a tree hugger," she laughed.

Kristi also shared how ordering new mulch for the playground had become a major headache. After seeing a checklist from the National Program for Playground Safety, she realized Winthrop needed several more inches. The custodian was slow to act and only placed the order after the third time she asked. In the meantime, Kristi's safety concerns prompted her to close the playground, which was very unpopular. Several days later, one hundred cubic yards of mulch arrived, but Kristi kept the playground closed because the cheap mulch ordered by the custodian was full of shredded pop cans and other dangerous items.

"Some of the same volunteers who helped install the playground equipment brought skid loaders to scoop it up and take it away. One of them blew a tire and asked the school to pay for it—a hundred and fifty bucks. The superintendent wouldn't do it! Can you believe that? So I'm paying for it out of our magazine-drive money."

"All that just for some mulch on the playground. I can say I've never once thought about that. I'm gonna look at my kids' playground tonight!" Sutt said.

Kristi was on a roll.

"And listen to what happened at our input conference the other night," she said. "We have this sixth-grade math teacher who is really old school, gives tons of homework, and has quite a reputation as an old bear. Her idea of multicultural education is using *Juan* instead of *John* for a math problem."

Kristi explained that the teacher and the mother of a sixth grader got into a shouting match when the teacher complained that parents give their kids too much help on homework. The mother countered that she has always monitored her children's homework completion and that helping her daughter with it was the only way she would get it all finished.

"The first thing I heard was the teacher ask if the mom intended to look over her daughter's shoulder in middle and high school," Kristi said. "Then the mom said, 'I plan to help my daughter succeed, which is more than I can say for you!' Then the teacher said something about thirty years of successful teaching. Finally the mom screamed something about her being a witch and shoved all her papers off the desk and walked out."

"Sure, why not!" Sutt exclaimed. "What did you do?"

"I went after the mom and tried to settle her down. Some teachers are saying I didn't support the teacher and should have helped her clean up and dealt with mom later. But others say the teacher loves to push parents' buttons and stir things up. She is kind of condescending."

Joe summarized his conclusions on the shop accident. "The super and associate super are coming down here tomorrow morning to decide what we're gonna do with the guy."

"Will he get fired?" Kristi asked. "The class sounds like a free-for-all."

"He's a goner," Sutt said. "Too much liability in the shop. Just think, Joe, if I wasn't in this job, I might have applied for the shop opening you're about to have! You'd be my boss!"

"Good God," Joe scoffed. "Look at what we've been talking about. I guess we know what Summers meant when he talked about reality calling. You won't find this stuff in a textbook."

That night, Joe shared their stories with Claire. For some reason, theirs were easier to share than his own.

"Those two are really good," he told Claire, as the late news ended.

"You're better," Claire countered. "Aren't you gonna watch the *Late Show*?"

Joe didn't answer, already drifting off.

QUESTIONS

1. Evaluate Joe's handling of the complaint about the crappy gram.
2. Evaluate Joe's handling of Brenton Michaels and Mark Watters.
3. Sort Joe's messages and emails into these categories: (1) issues that should be dealt with immediately; (2) issues that should be delegated to someone else; (3) issues that should go to the back burner; (4) leadership versus management.
4. What position should Joe take with Superintendent Zylstra and Associate Superintendent Mitchell regarding Merle Richards?

Chapter Nine

Mid-September

D-Day

WHAT NOW?

Joe arrived at school at 5:45 a.m.to shore up his office before the meeting with Zylstra and Mitchell. Not knowing how long it would take, he wanted to get some other things done in case he lost the entire morning. He and McHale had spent twenty minutes speculating on the position Zylstra would take when she and Mitchell walked into the outer office just after 7:00.

Joe offered coffee and invited them to take a seat at the round table in his office, where he had arranged folders with copies of his interview notes and an overall summary of his investigation. He'd also placed Richards's personnel file with twenty-some years' worth of evaluations in the center of the table.

"Since you're all early, I'd really like to cruise the building before we get started, just to be visible," Joe said, half-telling, half-asking. McHale nodded his approval.

"Absolutely," agreed Zylstra. "See you in ten minutes?"

When Joe returned, Zylstra began promptly by stating the purpose of the meeting was to come to agreement on what should happen with Richards. "It is safe to say that we're lucky—the student is lucky—this could have been catastrophic. Joe, we've seen your summary, but I'd like you to lead us through it."

Joe recounted the accident, including his failure to understand what Young meant when he said Bill had been "run over." This brought a chuckle from Mitchell and a roll of McHale's eyes. He talked about Bill apologizing for causing so much trouble and the call from union rep Herb Asbury. "Running scared," Mitchell mumbled.

Joe described his conversations with the students, which revealed minimal oversight from Richards. He noticed Zylstra's pained expression during this part of his description, as she thumbed through Richards's file. Finally, he explained how his conversation with Richards led him to believe supervision and management were virtually nonexistent.

When he finished, Zylstra spoke first. "We need to talk about next steps . . . all the way from trying to counsel him out to placing him on the evaluation cycle and watching him closely—*really closely*—to termination," she said. "I want everyone's take on this."

"Merle Richards is the classic example of a decent person being a horrible teacher," McHale said, adding that none of them would want him teaching their own children. "Our ultimate goal needs to be Pinicon High School without Merle Richards. It shouldn't have taken a near-tragic accident to get us to this point, but now that we're here, we have to jump on it."

Zylstra turned her eyes to Joe. "It's your building, Joe. What are your thoughts?"

Be assertive. Don't pull punches with members of your own team, he told himself. "You all know more about this stuff than I do, but I agree with Tom. There is no way I'd want him teaching my kids. The picture from the interviews is absolute chaos. He's clueless, horribly negligent, or both. If you can't get fired for running over a kid, what does it take?" Joe asked. "I mean, if this happens ten times, we've got serious injury or death eight or nine times."

The group drifted into hypothetical scenarios. What if Bill had been severely injured? What if Richards didn't have several years of favorable evaluations on file? What if Richards were a new teacher, rather than a veteran? What about the fire marshal's order to have Richards's area thoroughly cleaned or closed? Joe broke a long period of silence.

"Seems to me if Bill had been badly hurt or killed, God forbid, Richards would be history. Or if his parents were the kind who were going to sue the district."

"In that case, we tie Merle Richards's ass to a rocket and launch the sonofabitch," said Mitchell.

"And since they're *not*, Don?" McHale asked pointedly. "How is it any different?"

"Since they're not, this is a serious wake-up call. We put him on intensive improvement, watch him like a hawk. Maybe we can shore him up. If not, harass him into getting the hell out of here. It's on him," Mitchell said.

He continued: "You know the union will be all over this and turn it into a major fight. Termination, as pathetic as he sounds, is not the best option right now. I ran it by our attorney and he thinks we've got enough to do it, but I don't think the board has the cojones for it. So we scare him and Joe shores him up. That's better than setting off World War III. Maybe we can get him to leave, and if not, he at least runs a safer room."

McHale would have none of it. "I want you to picture the weakest teacher you can imagine. Lazy. Now put him in the shop with lots of dangerous equipment and some rough kids. You're gonna let the politics talk you out of terminating him? And you throw it on a rookie principal to fix him? He should have been out years ago and now's our chance."

"The board is a concern," Zylstra conceded. "I've informed them, but I don't have the relationship with them yet that Jerry Hughes had. They just don't trust Don and me enough yet."

"Convincing the board to do the right thing is your *job*, Carol. It has to start sometime," McHale said pointedly.

Joe could see Mitchell's jaw clinch.

"Tom, I understand that you and Joe have to live with Richards if he stays. I get that," Zylstra said.

"Do you also get that people will wonder what it takes to get fired here if he stays?" McHale countered, throwing up his hands. "The accident was too much. By the grace of God, Bill wasn't hurt or killed. This was Richards's fatal error," McHale said, slapping the table.

"Joe?" Zylstra prompted.

"I'm new and probably naïve. I can't see how he keeps his job. We fire a junior high football coach for a beer party, but Richards runs over a kid and stays? I'd have a hard time justifying that."

Mitchell let out a sigh. "I know how it feels at the building level. But I don't think a messy termination fight is something this shared superintendent arrangement can withstand right now. I don't wanna kick that hornet's nest if we don't have to."

"Sure, Don. *Let Joe do it* instead. Way to set the new guy up for success," McHale said, visibly disgusted.

"Goddammit Tom, I'm talking about a bigger picture here!" Mitchell countered before Zylstra hushed them both with her hands.

After a pause Zylstra spoke. "Let him twist a few more days, continued suspension with pay, pending the results of the investigation. Joe, the day after tomorrow, bring him in and tell him you anticipate that I will recommend that the board terminate him. Tell him I am confident the board will support my recommendation. Whether they actually will is another matter, but he doesn't know that. Maybe that will get him to quit. I'll poll the board members to see if they will go for termination. If so, he's out. If not, we'll put him on an intensive plan of assistance and try to counsel, supervise, or harass him out and hope for the best."

Alone in his office after the three had left, Joe's mind drifted back to Professor Summers warning how basing decisions on "what is good for kids" had become little more than a cliché. There was no way that Richards teaching industrial technology was good for kids. *If Summers was correct that the vast majority of teachers, unions, and boards were reasonable and unwilling to defend inexcusable behavior, then why were Zylstra and Mitchell so cautious? Did they lack the stomach for the fight? Or was there something else?*

He could feel his shoulders and neck tightening the way they always did when he was stressed. It was time to get out of the office and into the building. He needed a pick-me-up and to find the things that attracted him to the principalship in the first place.

STAGE SETTING

Joe had mixed emotions about starting formal teacher evaluations. On one hand, he was eager to fill his calendar with instructional-leadership activities and start showing himself as someone who knew something about instruction. He also hoped not so see any glaring problems. If Richards stayed, he would provide plenty. Starting the observation process in Joe's familiar curricular area—social studies—with Pat Patrazzo was as good a place to begin as any and Joe felt Patrazzo had plenty to work on.

Joe was surprised that the suggestion of a pre-observation conference seemed foreign to Patrazzo. "I'd rather you just show up. I'm a little better some days than others, but I can promise you I won't be doing anything special since you're in the room," he said.

Joe insisted the pre-observation conference was an essential part of the process, and they set a time during Patrazzo's planning time to discuss the upcoming U.S. history lesson, which focused on the lead up to the American Revolutionary War. Patrazzo handed Joe a photocopied plan from the teacher's edition of the text with a few notes written in the margins.

"So, give me the background here, Pat."

"The Boston Massacre. The book does a pretty good job of setting up how the colonists were fed up with the British and then things exploded."

"And so talk to me about your objectives and how it fits together with other lessons."

Patrazzo paused. "Well, it's right there in the book. It was a precursor to full-on war. The kids have been doing a timeline and map work. They should know the names, dates, and places."

"Okay. I think I heard an objective in there. Place the massacre in context and sequence; know the location and important people and their roles. Cause-and-effect stuff. Anything else?"

"Not really," Patrazzo said flatly.

"Okay, so let's talk specific strategies. How are you planning to get there?"

"Same way I usually do. Kids like a routine. Structure. I'm sure you understand that from coaching. They like to know what to expect. They are to come to class with their map work and timeline up to date. They know that a quiz is possible. If they have done the assigned reading and looked at the section review questions, they will be ready to discuss and check the homework."

Joe resisted the temptation to tell Patrazzo that he had just described the classic rip-and-read history lesson from every textbook in the country. Instead, he finished his notes and cut the pre-observation short, as things seemed to be going in circles, with Patrazzo speaking only when asked a direct question. "Fair enough, Pat. Is there anything else you want me to know or anything in particular you would like me to watch for when I come in?"

"I can't think of what it would be." Patrazzo said, sitting stoically in his chair.

QUESTIONS

1. Evaluate Joe's performance in the meeting about Merle Richards's future.

2. How should Superintendent Zylstra proceed with the Richards situation?

3. Evaluate Joe's handling of the pre-observation conference with Patrazzo.

Chapter Ten

Early October

The Unusual Is Routine

LEMONADE

The Pinicon School Board showed little interest in terminating Merle Richards, though Zylstra said she pushed the members as hard as she dared. As a result, the plan was for Joe to convince Richards that even a minor screw-up would mean the end for him. Joe couldn't tell what Richards thought. He had worked closely with Zylstra and McHale to develop a very specific plan of assistance for Richards aimed at safety and compliance but one that would not consume all of Joe's time.

McHale told Joe he was more disappointed than at any other time in his career, but that he hoped it might also be a good learning experience. The plan called for Richards to develop, post, and review specific safety procedures for all of his courses and demonstrate complete student compliance. His lesson plans were to be turned in one week in advance with notations of any procedures that involved heavy equipment, flammables, or anything particularly dangerous. Trouble was, Joe said, Richards's nonexistent discipline and awareness could render a box of paperclips dangerous.

Joe had been working hard to be present in every classroom every day, if only briefly. The plan placed him in Richards's shop for a formal observation each week and walkthroughs a couple of times a day. Richards appeared to be making a sincere effort to run a much tighter ship, though Young said

Richards's main problem was not related to effort, but rather ability: "I just don't think he has it in him."

MASSACRING THE MASSACRE

"The guy massacred the Boston Massacre," Joe told Kristi on the phone. "I mean, there is so much you could do with a lesson like that," he said, reflecting on some of the ideas he had jotted down to share with Patrazzo. He had tried to go into the observation with an open mind, even after the awkward pre-observation conference.

Patrazzo's students slogged through the forty-seven-minute period with all the enthusiasm of a forced march in the rain. Uphill. Patrazzo had a student take attendance and parked himself on a barstool behind his podium and began asking questions from the teacher's edition of the textbook. After about ten minutes of students parroting answers from the book, he told them to check their papers with their "red felt-tip pen." Apparently no other types of pens were permitted.

Following this, Patrazzo used a laser pointer to refer to an illustrated timeline on white boards at the side of the room. The student-produced timeline was a bright spot for Joe, as it was student-created and featured illustrated colonial scenes. "It was so boring I wanted to intervene. I mean, *I* was bored and I like history," he said.

"Are you gonna tell him that and share your ideas?" Kristi asked.

"I don't know. Maybe I'll try, but I'm pretty sure he thinks it was good stuff. He says I'm welcome to come in anytime, but don't most teachers do something good when they're being observed? If that was his A-game, I can't imagine what it's like on a bad day."

Kristi advised that since this was the first formal observation Joe had conducted, he needed to play his hand thoughtfully. He needed to be honest and direct, without alienating Patrazzo. "You know he's gonna talk about the way you handle the whole process, so make sure you get your points across, but be careful. And he's a member of your leadership team, so he has some influence."

Joe agreed, thanked her, and promised to call her after the post-observation conference. He smiled as he hung up the phone. McHale's advice was nearly identical, cautioning him against getting frustrated with Patrazzo's low energy and nonchalant approach. "You've got to focus on his skills and capacity as a teacher. It's very possible what you saw is all he knows how to do. So you're gonna have to show the way," McHale urged.

RECLAIMING AN AGENDA OR JUGGLING?

By mid-October, Joe had settled into a routine. He typically arrived at school at 6:30 a.m., taking the long way through the building, gym, locker rooms, and auditorium, often stopping in the weight room to chat and getting a boiler-room joke from custodian Dave Crawford. Fall sports, particularly football, were off to a good start. Discipline referrals were slightly below the same point in the previous year, though Joe questioned the accuracy of the records. Attendance, which he knew was accurate, was up slightly. He knew all of the students by name and had begun meeting regularly with the student council, which seemed pleased to have his attention. He shared all of this news in his Friday blog update and listed upcoming events and pointed out highlights he had seen during the week.

The leadership team was up and running and seemed to be embracing the role Joe had given it: to provide teacher input and ideas to the most pressing issues at Pinicon Secondary, especially those related to learning. He called it an "open door, open mind" policy. Most members chosen had been the same ones Joe would have picked, with one surprising exception—Pat Patrazzo. McHale said he hoped the mission wasn't too broad and that Patrazzo wouldn't influence the team to undermine Joe. "There must be some reason teachers wanted Patrazzo on the team. I have to respect that and maybe I can capitalize on whatever it is," Joe said.

REFLECTING AND DEFINING

He was working hard to maintain a daily routine that included more than surviving the endless stream of interruptions and unplanned things. Claire was constantly after him to take time for himself during the day. "You've got to eat, take a breath, and find some things that refresh you a little. I'm worried that you're overworking right now."

To that end, Joe had found that an early morning three-mile run helped him start the day fresh. It was also when he did his best thinking. He realized that "the Pinicon Way" slogan appeared everywhere, but beyond the tradition of hard-hitting football teams, no one could define what it really meant, including the leadership team. Mark Watters, seemingly still bothered by the way Joe handled Brenton Michaels and the stache/stash situation, said in a leadership team meeting, "*A lot* of things need defining around here."

The leadership team agreed that defining the Pinicon Way was a good professional learning goal for the building. Joe shared the plan with staff via his Pirate's Voice blog:

> Hello Pirates!
>
> I will admit that I've been hustling to keep up, and posting to the Pirate Voice has been difficult, but let me share a few thoughts.
>
> A few weeks into the school year, it is easy to see why we have a number of new students at Pinicon. I know you'll continue to welcome them and help them become immersed in everything that makes this such a great place to live and learn. Special thanks also to Jeralyn Kramer and the Pinicon Pals for their help with the transition.
>
> Far and away, the best part of my job is spending time in your classrooms. Even though I haven't been there as much as I would like, I've learned a number of things, including:
>
> - that we have a creative and dedicated group of teachers who are working hard to engage our capable students, and
> - that I have a lot to learn about how to best help teachers and students, in addition to learning more about lots of content and our curriculum.
>
> Thanks to Martha Mills for her extra work getting the new laptop cart ready. I know how disappointed everyone must have been when the water leak ruined the equipment last year. Thanks to our insurance company, the new computers are nearly ready to roll.
>
> As you may know, I'm a runner, though not a fast one. I find that I feel better, I am more alert, and it relieves stress (not that we educators have much). I also find that it gives me time and space to think. It struck me the other morning that "the Pinicon Way" is such an important part of the culture here, yet exactly what it means has not been defined.
>
> I've raised this with the leadership team, which agrees this is a valuable way for us to spend some professional learning time. So, in the coming months, we'll be working to define what "the Pinicon Way" means. At the very least, this will help me better understand our school's culture. At the very most, it will guide the way we teach, learn, and support each other.
>
> Hope to see everyone at a Pinicon activity/event very soon. Thanks for all you do!

Joe felt himself settling into a smoother routine during the next couple of weeks. He'd had more good days than bad, although Professor Summers had cautioned against tracking them in those terms. "You've got to take the long view of this job. It's a marathon, not a sprint," he cautioned. "Count the seeds you planted, not the crops you harvested today."

WAYLAID

It was unusual for a bus driver to call Joe on the radio, unless it was an early morning check to see if Joe had donuts in his office for them—something he had arranged for the final Friday of every month. Joe assumed there was a problem when he was summoned to one of the buses after school had been dismissed. "Be right there," he told the driver.

Outside the bus, Joe saw bus driver Ernie Johansen and a teacher's aide tending to Henry Miller, whose hair was stuck to his bright-red face by a mixture of sweat and blood. Henry, a meek seventh grader, was easy to miss. He was painfully shy and wasn't involved in much.

"That one right here just waylaid him," Ernie said, pointing to Mace Stallworth, who was leaning against a retaining wall, casts on both arms up to his elbows. "Got on the bus and punched him five or six times before I got to him."

Joe called the nurse's office, forgetting that Rose Johnson went home at 2:30. Joe asked Jeralyn to tend to Henry and call his parents. When he began asking students what happened, several trustworthy kids verified Ernie's account. "He just went off for no reason, Mr. Gentry. The kid's crazy. Henry was just sitting there looking at a magazine."

Joe had wondered about Mace, a lanky freshman who had not been listed on the initial list of Kessler transfers. He had been assigned a Pinicon Pal, though it was obvious that he wanted nothing to do with the program. June Ramsey, Mace's special-education teacher, described him as "such an angry boy."

Joe started interrogating Mace on the sidewalk instead of taking him to his office. When asked what started the incident, Mace shrugged and said Henry had looked at him stupid.

"He looked at you stupid?" Joe asked.

"Always does. I told him he better not be staring at me like a little fag."

"Mace, you've got hard casts on both arms. Those are like weapons. And Henry's a seventh grader. Everyone tells me he was reading a magazine minding his own business."

"Whatever. All anyone does in this fucking school is look at me."

"Lose the mouth. You're in enough trouble already," Joe said.

"Whatever. When can I go?"

"I'll tell you when you can go," Joe hissed, leaning into Mace. "I don't know what is going on with you, but it's about to end."

Joe walked Mace to his office and dialed the number listed for Mace's mother. "I'm going to put you on speakerphone so you can tell her what's going on." His mother didn't answer and the phone didn't roll over to voicemail. The alternate number was disconnected. Joe let Mace sit in the detention room for about an hour and, after a few more attempts, Joe drove him home.

He was glad to see a car parked outside Mace's trailer in the rundown Pleasant Acres Mobile Home Park. His mother, Lorna, was seated on a massive velour sofa with *Jeopardy* blaring on the television. She stayed seated as Joe followed Mace into the trailer, which was strewn with dirty clothes, pizza boxes, and soda and beer cans. "What did you go and do now?" she asked her son.

"Hit some kid who was looking at me."

"Shit. It figures," she said. "You the cops?" she asked Joe.

"No, I'm Joe Gentry, the principal," he said, carefully stepping over a hole in the floor.

Joe explained what had happened and that Mace would be in-school suspended. He had been leaning toward suspending him out of school for a few days, but the dismal condition of their trailer changed his mind.

"Boy's half-crazy," his mom said, gesturing toward a three-foot-wide hole in the living room wall. "He done that when I told him to take out the trash. That's how he got them casts. Busted both wrists."

Mace had disappeared to the back of the trailer. Joe asked his mother to step outside so they could talk. As she rose to go outside with him, Joe saw that she was more gaunt than he realized and covered with scabs, which she picked at while they stood in the driveway. Joe said Mace had apparently attacked Henry for no reason. "I can believe that. He's got no reason for anything. I can't control him."

"So you thought transferring schools might help?"

"Nothing helps. They just said that's where he was going."

Joe paused, wondering what she meant, but didn't ask. They talked a while longer, long enough for Joe to hear a sad family history of abuse, unemployment, and dysfunction. He said he wanted to suspend Mace in school so his schoolwork could be monitored but that he was kicked off the bus indefinitely.

"That's fine but I got no license and can't get him there. It's better he ain't here because we been goin' at it pretty good. You seen the wall. And now this. Boy's gonna end up dead or in prison like his dad."

Joe said he would try to arrange transportation. "You didn't answer your phone when I called earlier. Will you answer when I call about what happens next?"

"Write down the number. I don't answer unless I recognize the number."

On the way back to Pinicon, Joe thought about Mace and other tough kids he'd known. *It's a wonder they don't cause more trouble than they do, given their backgrounds*, he thought. Mace seemed like that kind of kid. Hanging out at home for several days was a bad idea. Keeping him at school might not be much better, but he could at least be monitored. The question was how to get him there.

Joe's conversation with Henry Miller's mother went better than expected. Henry had no broken bones but two black eyes and nine stitches. "It will all heal. I just don't understand. Henry didn't *do* anything. I want to know what is being done with the other boy, Mace."

Joe explained that he had met with Mace's mother and that Mace would be disciplined. "I don't want to seem secretive, but I can't discuss that with you, in the same way that I can't talk about Henry to another parent. I hope you can understand that. But rest assured that this will be handled according to our policy. This is not something we see as boys being boys. It is serious and we will treat it as such."

Mrs. Miller seemed satisfied, though Joe still didn't know exactly what to do with the suspension and Mace's transportation. He dialed Kristi, hoping her special-education background would help. Like Lorna, she didn't answer. Unlike Lorna's, her phone rolled over to voicemail.

PATRAZZO POST-OBS

The post-observation conference with Patrazzo had been difficult to arrange, mostly because of Joe's schedule—attending several curriculum meetings in Kessler with Zylstra and Mitchell, dealing with a handful of student issues, and struggling with a confusing State Department of Education website for reporting enrollment.

"I think of these like a post-game film session," Joe said, hoping the sports reference connected with Patrazzo, who was a sports guy.

"How many have you done?" Patrazzo asked. "This is the first time you've been principal, right?"

Patrazzo was dull, but Joe caught the subtle shot at his credibility. Patrazzo knew damn well he was a first-time principal.

"I haven't done a lot of formal observations, but I have spent a ton of hours observing teachers and talking about ways to improve," he said, wishing he had something stronger.

"Just trying to establish the credibility of the witness," Patrazzo said smugly.

"Right. So, how do you think the lesson went?" he asked, torn between the allure of some verbal jousting and remaining steadfastly professional. Patrazzo didn't make it easy.

"Isn't it about how *you* think it went? You're the expert evaluator."

Joe paused. *What kind of teacher would Patrazzo be if he put the same energy into teaching that he put into being glib and cantankerous?* "It's partially about the judgments I make related to artifacts and observations. And state standards, of course. But I've always thought teachers grow through self-reflection and their own desire to improve, not something the principal says," he said, again resisting sarcasm.

"So you've *always* thought that? For the couple of months you've been principal?" Patrazzo asked in a voice dripping with condescension.

This guy is unreal, Joe thought. "Pat, I'd like to have a meaningful conversation with you about the lesson I observed. You seem more interested in talking about my inexperience as principal. You may see me as unqualified or worse. But until the board shares your opinion, I'm here. I hope you'll be respectful of our time so we can use it to benefit kids and your teaching."

Patrazzo showed no sign of backing off. "No need to be defensive. I'm just trying to get a frame of reference. I'm fascinated that someone of your age and experience is a teaching expert. I can't wait to hear what they taught you in principal camp."

Joe was done. "One thing they taught me is that some people are more ready for conversation than others. You know that sign on your podium? The one about having the courage to believe the truth? Let me tell you the truth. What you're doing is bullshit and a waste of our time. I don't like wasting time. I'll give you a write-up of my observations and I hope you'll be ready to talk about them as a professional sometime soon," he said, standing and gesturing toward his office door, realizing how awkward it felt to be directing someone out of his office.

Patrazzo was unrelenting. "You're using profanity but *I'm* the one being unprofessional? This is a little different."

"It is what it is, Pat. You don't seem very interested in the process."

Joe's adrenaline pumped as he made his rounds through the building. Patrazzo was obviously testing him and Joe had taken the bait and let Patrazzo under his skin. *Why the hell had the teachers chosen him to be on the leadership team?* Maybe Joe had shown that he wasn't a pushover. Maybe he earned a little of Patrazzo's respect by standing up to him. Or maybe Joe was just trying to make himself feel better. It was hard to know.

He began thinking about the timing of the exchange. The leadership team would soon begin facilitating the effort to define the Pinicon Way. Kristi had warned that the way Joe handled this first formal observation would spread through the faculty. He shuddered to think of Patrazzo's description in the faculty lounge. If Patrazzo went on about how the principal had "cussed him out," Joe was in trouble. On the other hand, maybe some would appreciate that Joe stood up to him. He wished he had the whole meeting to do over.

"I just screwed up royally," he told McHale on the phone. McHale agreed that Patrazzo was clearly challenging him and that Joe had lost his cool. "I'm sure he loved getting under your skin, but I suspect he realizes you're not a wuss."

"Even so, I feel really stupid and like I violated my own four rules. The honesty, respect, responsibility, and courtesy stuff I talked about on the first day."

"Well, yeah. You fell a little short there," McHale conceded. "But don't beat yourself up too much. Just think about how you can regain the upper hand and the high ground."

AN INVITATION

Joe was pleased when Helen McCallister, a Pinicon English teacher of some twenty years, stuck her head into his office.

"You said you were going to be looking for opportunities to get into our classrooms and learn along with teachers and students, correct?"

"Absolutely, Helen. Do you have something for me?" Joe asked.

"I may have an opportunity for you."

McCallister had updated the reading list for her Great Books course and was including Tim O'Brien's (1990) Vietnam War story, *The Things They Carried.* "I'd like to invite members of the community who served in Vietnam to read the book along with our class and join the discussions, to the extent that they're available. Maybe you would like to also."

Joe grinned. "Helen, I would *love to.* What a fabulous idea. Thank you so much for asking me. Would you mind if I included this in my blog and the column I write for the newspaper?"

She nodded and produced a purchase order for additional copies of the book. "Thank you. I look forward to your contributions," she said.

DÉTENTE

The next morning Joe was struggling through a stack of forms that were apparently overdue to the Kessler Central Office when he heard Patrazzo's trademark whistling in the outer office. Patrazzo tapped lightly on Joe's office door. "May I speak with you a minute?" he asked.

Joe invited him in, still uncomfortable with the way the post-observation had ended and unsure of how to move forward. Claire had told him his actions were fine, "up to the point where you said bullshit." She had advised letting a little time go by and then stopping by his classroom to apologize and restart the conversation. That, coupled with an acknowledgment that Patrazzo did have a wealth of historical content knowledge, seemed like a good approach.

Joe greeted him with a neutral-sounding "good morning." Patrazzo dropped a Pinicon School District Grievance Form on Joe's desk. "I've replayed our meeting in my mind and filled out the grievance form, which is something I've never done before."

Joe resisted the temptation to scan the form. Just then, Carrie walked in. "Excuse me, Mr. Gentry, but Lorna Stallworth is on the phone. She said you were to be bringing Mace to school. Is that right?"

Joe had forgotten that he was to be getting Mace to school or find someone else to do it since he was suspended from the buses. "Tell her I'll be there as soon as I can. Or someone will." Joe would be a high-priced chauffer if he brought Mace to school. And yet he wasn't sure who else could do it, and he didn't want Mace sitting at home. *Forget Mace for now*, he thought.

BACK TO PATRAZZO

He was dying to know how bad the grievance form made him look, but held Patrazzo's eyes. "Your swearing at me was unprofessional, inappropriate, and certainly grievable. But I had a change of heart and won't be filing it."

Joe caught Patrazzo's arm as he turned to leave. "Pat, you're right. I kind of lost it and responded unprofessionally. I violated my own principles and need to apologize, too. I *am* sorry," he said, offering a handshake.

Patrazzo looked at Joe and nodded slightly. "Thank you for that," he said, taking Joe's hand. "But I'm *not apologizing*. I'm just *not filing the grievance*."

Patrazzo, while seeming contrite, had not used the word *sorry*. As he turned to leave, he looked back at Joe. "Let's call it détente. You're a social studies guy. Look it up."

QUESTIONS

1. How should Joe approach the situation with Merle Richards, given the superintendent's decision?
2. What kinds of issues should Joe address through his blog and what should be handled face to face?
3. Evaluate Joe's handling of the Mace Stallworth and Henry Miller incident. What should his next steps be?
4. Joe is pleased to receive the invitation to Helen McCallister's class. What other practical ways might he use to become involved in classrooms?
5. Evaluate Joe's interaction with Pat Patrazzo. What should happen next?

Chapter Eleven

Mid-October

Definitions and Personalities

SLOGANS, GUIDES, AND PERSPECTIVES

Joe wondered if assembling the faculty and most of the support staff to begin defining "the Pinicon Way" so close to homecoming was a good idea. On the other hand, he thought it might send the message that homecoming shouldn't completely derail the daily operation of the school. Plus, the leadership team seemed eager to start.

Joe welcomed everyone, reminding them that he preferred the term *professional learning* to *professional development* or *in-service*. He reinforced his plan that nonurgent, managerial issues would be addressed on his blog and that staff should develop the habit of checking it, just as they did the daily announcements.

"You know I like questions like whether our school is mostly about teaching or learning," he said. "Defining the Pinicon Way, while perhaps messy, may be the most important thing we'll do together this year, and I thank the leadership team in advance for leading the process."

Before Joe could continue, Stu Petersen spoke up. "Before we start the in-service, a lot of us want to know what's happening with Mace Stallworth and the bus incident."

Joe was tempted to correct him on the use of the term *in-service*, but let it go. He had anticipated the question and updated his blog with a summary of what was being done. "Stu, I've updated my blog with everything I can tell

99

you about it. This is an example of how I want to protect our professional learning time but still give you the information you need."

"We think it is something we ought to talk about as a faculty. It's a safety concern."

"I appreciate that. And I'm willing to have that conversation, but not now. I can tell you that Mace has been suspended, in-school, for five days and indefinitely from the bus."

He wondered if sharing even that much information negated his intention to protect professional learning time. Joe assumed the teachers who were whispering to each other wanted to discuss the incident, but he decided that giving it any more attention would detract from their professional learning, so he pushed on.

"In our time together today, I want to start the process of defining what the Pinicon Way really is. For some, it is probably a catchy slogan. For others, I suspect it means something pretty specific. Some of you know it when you see it. I think it was Supreme Court Justice Potter Stewart who said he didn't have a definition of *obscenity*, but knew it when he saw it. It's important that we all share an understanding of what the Pinicon Way means, beyond slogans. It should guide everything we do."

Mark Watters's hand popped up. Joe nodded.

"Are you suggesting that the Pinicon Way is just a T-shirt slogan?"

"Not at all, Mark," Joe said, trying not to sound defensive. "If you re-member my blog, I said it should guide everything we do. The way we teach, the way we interact with students and each other. The clearer we are on what it means, the better off we're going to be."

Joe said he had no intention of imposing his own view of what the Pinicon Way meant. "We may not be in complete agreement on every detail. We have different styles, experiences, and backgrounds. It sounds cliché, but I see those differences as strengths. At the end of this process, I'd like us to have a clearer picture of what we're about as a learning community. Something we can agree to live by. The Pinicon Way of teaching, learning, work-ing together." Finally, he explained that the ferreting out of these definitions would be time consuming and difficult at times. He stressed the importance of an honest and respectful exchange of ideas, reminding them that the pro-cess was as important as the results.

Joe turned the session over to Rhonda Prior and Patrazzo, whom the leadership team had chosen to facilitate. Prior led a brainstorming session, followed by a questioning exercise they titled "The Five Whys." After several minutes of small-group discussion, they reconvened the full group, asking for a list of strengths from each table, which Patrazzo recorded on a white board. Allison Jesup drew the biggest laugh of the day when she asked if she was the only one who couldn't read Patrazzo's writing.

"Ooooh, Pat? Are you gonna take that from a rookie?" asked Martha Mills.

"Only because it's true," Patrazzo deadpanned to uproarious laughter, tossing the marker to Prior.

Joe was pleased with the levity and that he had been able to fade into the background during discussions. Rather than participating directly, he circulated around the room, listening carefully to each group. He was pleasantly surprised that an hour passed quickly and produced a long list with many similarities. Joe made his way back to the front of the room.

"Thanks for your effort today. This is a great start. I've already got a better handle on some of the things that make Pinicon great. Thanks to Rhonda and Pat for facilitating this first effort. Let's give them a hand along with the coaches who arranged to delay the start of practice, rather than missing the session. It speaks volumes," he said. "Finally, I want to acknowledge the presence of our support staff in this effort. They're an essential part of this team effort."

The meeting broke up as Den Herder and the other coaches hustled out of the room. Merle Richards shuffled out in his usual tortoise-like way. Stu Petersen cackled in the back of the room, most likely at his own off-color joke. Some continued talking about the exercise and perceived strengths of the school, while others talked about kids, ball games, or weekend plans. But they were talking. Joe remembered Susan Scott's (2004) statement from *Fierce Conversations*: "The conversation *is* the relationship." He smiled.

Back in his office, he tidied his desk, slid the window shut, and turned out the light. It was an early end to what felt like a productive day. If this was what establishing some norms and developing a learning community felt like, he could handle more of it, especially with headaches from Merle Richards, Mace Stallworth, Patrazzo, and homecoming on the horizon.

SKYPE CONFERENCE

With Margaret tucked into bed, Elliott watching football on TV, and Claire reading, Joe decided to see if Sutt and Kristi were at their computers. He wanted to share the Pinicon Way session and ask for advice on Mace Stallworth. He smiled when both appeared on the screen.

"Finally, one of us is doing something close to instructional leadership!" Kristi said.

"You better enjoy it, 'cause homecoming's next and then it's all over," Sutt cautioned.

Kristi reminded Joe to look at Mace's IEP to determine if what happened was related to his disability. "Depending on the answer, it all goes from there. Have you looked at his IEP?"

Joe said Mace's IEP called only for a couple of periods a day in the resource room.

"If he hasn't had other blow-ups, maybe it's an isolated deal. Go around and ask what his teachers have seen. The best predictor of future behavior is the past."

Joe agreed and said a more pressing problem might be how to get Mace to school, since he was not returning to the bus anytime soon.

"I know you can't spend your time shuttling him," she said. "Can Kessler do it?"

"I'd go another way, Joe," said Sutt. "The last thing the kid needs is more bad experience with Kessler. You're probably the first school guy to show up at home. Maybe you can build some rapport with mom and even the kid. Tell him you'll be there to haul his ass out of bed and get him to school, at least during the suspension, and see how it goes. What is it, like ten miles? It might make a connection and show that you really want to help."

Joe was intrigued at his two friends' suggestions, different though they were.

Kristi asked for help on a volunteer issue. She said a long-time volunteer known as Big Wanda was spending uninvited and unnecessary time at the elementary school, even though her kids had moved on to middle and high school.

"Mostly she's in the way and eating all the food. And she eats more than you, Sutt."

"Let's not get crazy with it, Kristi," Joe chimed. "She *can't* eat more than Sutt."

"I'm serious. She gorges herself. I think she has an eating disorder. We almost ran out at the teacher appreciation lunch." Kristi said the previous principal didn't have the heart to tell her she was disrupting things or eating too much.

Joe asked if the family needed food assistance. "Quite the contrary. They've got all kinds of money. I think it's an obsessive/compulsive thing—the food and the volunteering."

"Why don't you just tell her that she's not needed and to quit taking all the food? Just say it," Sutt suggested. "She's not gonna figure it out on her own."

"Tell her she's taking volunteer spots of parents with kids in the building. And see what the counselor thinks about an eating disorder."

"I guess I have been wanting to avoid it and feeling sorry for her," Kristi admitted.

Next she reported that the construction work was virtually complete. "I've actually developed a decent relationship with the construction guys. I was out there a lot gently talking about deadlines, but they had a hard time hearing that from a woman."

"So what did you do?" Sutt asked.

He and Joe laughed out loud at her answer. "I went to my default—spreadsheets. I hung color-coded, poster-sized spreadsheets of what was left to do, what needed to be rechecked, and what was done. It made all the difference in the world. The other day I went out there and they had made a big sign that said, 'We love our bulldog,' with my picture on it. Can you believe that? Someone calling me a bulldog? Anyway, it's been great since then."

"Being called a bulldog is a lot better than most of the alternatives," Sutt said.

"Sounds like they were just waiting for you to be more assertive. And they knew you weren't going to go away," said Joe. "One of them will probably ask you out!"

"Funny. One more to share. I bet you guys would be interested in this at the secondary level." She said that asking teachers about zeros and to explain their grading scales had become unexpectedly controversial. "We're all over the place—points, plain letter grades, points for effort, points for putting your name on the paper, others not giving any points unless everything is done a certain way. More complicated than the tax code."

"Rudy said they did a form of No Zeros at his old school. They studied it for a year and wound up not giving zeros," Sutt said.

They debated the merits of a no-zeros policy before Sutt changed the subject. "I can beat both of you for the best story this time," he announced. "Last football game. We're on the road at Truman High. There's a tradition where kids from both schools dress up in costumes. The student councils organize it together and it raises some money for the food bank. Get this! I'm eating a piece of pizza with the assistant from Truman and I see Darth Vader drop his costume at the ten-yard line and take off across the field. The dude is bare naked except for the mask and light saber. We take off after him. He stops at the fifty and does a hip thrust and takes off again. Crowd going crazy, other administrators are starting to chase him now. Plus the cops."

Joe and Kristi howled.

"We're closing in on him when he jumps a fence, dives into a minivan, and they're gone."

"How does a stud like you let him get away, Sutt? I'm really disappointed!" Kristi said.

"My pants got caught on the fence and I tore the hell out of my leg. Sixteen stitches and a tetanus shot. Ruined my new pants."

"Did you catch him?" Joe asked.

"Some parents wrote down the license plate number, and the cops caught them twenty minutes later. It turns out the kid is from Oswald, a junior. Never had an office referral. On the quiz bowl team. The streaker is a freaking *mathlete*! I love this job!"

"And the tough-guy assistant principal winds up with stitches from chasing him!" Kristi laughed.

INFLUENCE AND ENTITLEMENT

Susan Shottenkirk was as close as there was to Pinicon royalty. She had been homecoming queen in high school and later married into an affluent family that made its fortune selling tires and appliances. Though the company had expanded to several states, family ties kept Shottenkirk Tire and Appliance headquarters in Pinicon. The all-weather track and a lot of technology for teachers were testaments to the family's generosity. The downside was that Susan seemed to expect special treatment.

Joe's casual conversations with her had been pleasant enough. He wondered if the appointment she had scheduled was to explore a new donation the family wanted to make. *Jeez, I am thinking like an administrator*, Joe admonished himself.

He welcomed Susan to his office. "I've waited as long as I could," she said.

"Sounds like something's on your mind. How can I help?"

Susan said the best thing about Pinicon had always been a tremendous sense of pride and community. "That's why we've kept our offices here and are strong supporters of the school."

Joe agreed. "You bet. Those are the same things that drew Claire and me to Pinicon."

Susan said she had been asked to raise a couple of issues as president of the Pirate Booster Club. She noted that the football team was undefeated and on a roll, but despite that, some long-time Pinicon families were feeling disillusioned and overlooked. She said many members had complained that Pinicon was losing its identity.

Joe wasn't sure where she was headed and asked for clarification.

She offered a litany of concerns, from free sports physicals for Kessler transfers to newcomers getting special guides and attention from the principal, and some of the transfer kids being troublemakers. Although she never mentioned it, Joe knew playing time was also an issue. He addressed her concerns one at a time, noting that the free physicals were available to anyone who needed help paying and that ensuring new students' smooth transition into Pinicon was important. He let the troublemakers comment slide.

"Were the free physicals made available to *Pinicon* kids?" she asked.

Joe paused. "The way I see it, *all* kids participating in Pinicon activities are Pinicon kids."

"A lot of people feel like special privileges have been extended to the Kessler kids. And of course, when they took some of the starting spots on the teams . . . well, that didn't help. And then they get this special buddy system. Aren't we bending over backward a little too far here?"

Joe didn't have time for this. "Concerns about playing time should go to the coach or Frank Young. I would hope people would be thrilled to have their kids in a school with great facilities and teachers and strong programs in athletics, the arts, you name it. No wonder people want to come here. It is my job to build on those things and welcome newcomers."

"But that shouldn't come at the expense of kids who have been here all along and paid their dues! Some of these new kids act like they own the place and have taken over," Susan protested, more firmly. "You may be unaware, but there's a real perception of favoritism."

"I appreciate you letting me know," Joe said, rising to walk Susan toward the door. "I can assure you that I'm principal for *all* our students, not certain ones. And if you know of folks who would like to visit with me—about issues other than playing time—please have them contact me."

"We just want you to be successful here," she said, extending her hand for a more emphatic than expected handshake.

Young assured Joe that the visit was mostly about Susan's insatiable desire to feel important. "How about the irony of Susan Shottenkirk bitching about kids getting special treatment when that's what she's expected for thirty years! Priceless. Did she get into us firing Seth Larson?" Young asked.

"No, why?"

"You know Seth is her nephew, right?"

"Ohhh. No, I didn't know that."

"A little history for you. We fired poor Seth. Now some kids like Javaris Hayes come to town and some of their kids aren't the big fish anymore. Does she know the team is *winning*? Some of them would rather have their kids playing all the time on a losing team. Might make for an interesting homecoming, chief," Young said, eyebrows raised.

THE RECESS QUARTERBACK

"I'm glad I caught you," Kristi said into her phone. "I need some advice. I don't want to ask my super because I don't want to look like I don't know what to do."

"Perfect. Maybe I can solve some of your problems, since I don't know what to do with mine," Joe said. "What's up?"

Kristi said a respected fourth-grade teacher with ten years of experience at Winthrop had complained that a new fifth-grade teacher, one of only three men in the building, was playing football with students at recess.

"Kristi, I'm a secondary guy, but I'm not seeing the problem. What's the catch?"

"The catch is that our contract says that the *associates* do recess duty, not teachers."

"If he wants to go out for recess, who cares?"

Kristi said the issue had angered many veteran teachers, who said they had fought long and hard to free teachers from recess duty in order to create time for teacher collaboration. She said the teacher was actively collaborating with other teachers and she was aware of no problems, other than the reaction of some.

"I told her I would talk to him about it, but that I was more interested in teaching and learning. The truth is I thought it was great that he wants to play with the kids. Recess office referrals are down and the kids love him. I never thought this would be a problem."

"I'd let him know the history of teachers fighting for the collaboration time and that some of his colleagues are upset. Then I'd let them collaborate their way out of it. And I'd tell him to keep up the role-modeling with kids. Hey, I've got to run to a meeting with the homecoming committee. Let me know how it goes, okay?"

"Gotcha, Joe. Thanks. I love that we can do this. It helps."

IT'S A HISTORICAL SYMBOL

"I hate to ruin your lunch conversation with these fine young ladies," Jeralyn said as Joe sat amid a group of sophomore girls. At first, students had been taken aback when Joe began joining their lunch groups, but since had begun asking him when he would join theirs.

"I want to tell you about a little transaction that happened in a bathroom," she said.

Joe raised an eyebrow. "That can't be good."

"Some kids told me that Dan Arstman sold Cooper McDermott a Confederate flag in the bathroom."

Joe sighed. "Repeat that back to yourself. Some schools are dealing with ecstasy and assaults in the bathroom. We're chasing Confederate flag sales."

"I know it's funny in a backwater kind of way, but it shows we have issues that need attention," she said, referencing her earlier warnings about ethnic tension at Pinicon. She could see the wheels turning in Joe's head.

"You're probably right."

That afternoon, Joe talked with Dan Arstman and Cooper McDermott, neither of whom had a single office referral, about their transaction. When Joe called the wide-eyed boys to his office to ask why they handled the sale out in the bathroom, both said they thought some people would be upset.

"Like who?" Joe asked.

"Well, mainly the Kessler kids. The black kids, I guess," Dan answered.

"Should they be upset?" Joe asked.

"No. It's just something from history."

"What do you guys think of when you see the Confederate flag?"

The two mentioned everything from rock and roll to hunting, fishing, and four-wheel-drive trucks. Then Joe asked if they could think of things about the flag that might be upsetting to people. "Well, the Civil War and stuff. Like, slavery, but that was like, a hundred and some years ago," Dan said.

Joe remembered a demonstration he had seen Professor Summers do in class. He pulled a small beach ball given to him by a textbook vendor out of his desk drawer and blew it up. He held it up and asked the boys to tell him what they saw. They glanced at each other, curiously.

"A beach ball," Dan said.

"No, the colors you see. Describe the ball," Joe corrected.

"Oh. White, blue, and orange," Cooper said.

Joe paused for effect. "Cooper, what are you talking about? I'm holding it right here and it's yellow, red, and green. Duh."

The boys shook their heads, eyes squinting. Joe turned the ball around. "Like I said, boys, yellow, red, and green. What you see depends on your perspective. To you, the flag means rock and roll, the great outdoors, and a nice pickup. To a lot of others, a lot of African American folks, it's about slavery, torture, and hate. That may not be what you see, but it's what others see. Does that make any sense?"

"Well, kind of, but we're not saying anything bad. We just like the flag," Dan insisted.

"I get that. And that's why you're not in trouble. I think you guys have been straight with me. But I don't want to see the flag at school and I don't want you selling *anything* in my bathrooms. No flags, no shirts, no candy. Nothing. That's how rumors get started. Got that?"

MAMA BEAR

He had hung up from talking with Lieutenant Beckworth at the Pinicon Police Department about some extra eyes on the building at night with homecoming looming when Carrie buzzed in. "Joe, Mrs. Rolling is here to see you if you have a minute."

"Sure," Joe answered, dropping his highlighter and struck by the irony that he was only two paragraphs into an article about principals balancing their time. *Now there's a blog topic*, he thought. He remembered Professor Summers's claim that principals saying they have no time for professional reading was a copout. "What you're really saying if you adhere to that is that the job is running you, instead of you running the job." He wanted to agree with the professor, but hadn't managed much time for professional reading yet.

"I'm Joe Gentry, Mrs. Rolling. Nice to meet you. How can I help you?"

Janelle Rolling got right to the point. "My son, Travis, is a freshman. And your PE teacher, Mr. Petersen, has successfully ruined the start of high school," she said, voice already shaking. "A lot of us have been through this with him."

"Okay," Joe said, "I'm glad you're here. Can you tell me some specifics?"

Mrs. Rolling said Stu Petersen had "berated and humiliated" her son in PE, causing him to cry in front of his classmates. "It's bad enough to have a teacher climbing all over you constantly, but to make you cry in front of your classmates is even worse," she said, dabbing at tears. "We've got all this emphasis on bullies. What about when it's the teacher?"

Joe slid a box of tissue across the circular table in his office. "Do you have any idea what was going on? This is the first I've heard of it."

"Oh, I'm sure it is the first you've heard, but it won't be the last if that asshole doesn't back off his power trip with my son!"

"I can see you're upset, but if I'm going to be any help at all, I need to understand Travis's side of what was going on."

"First of all, Travis is not a jock and Petersen has no use for boys who aren't in sports." She said Travis was standing around at the end of class when Petersen "just started in on him."

"I should back up and ask if you've talked with Mr. Petersen about this," Joe asked.

"Not this time. We've been down that road and have watched others try. This guy gets off on humiliating kids and he's not gonna do it with Travis!" she shrieked.

After a few more minutes, Joe realized she was becoming more upset, not less, and that he'd probably gotten all he was going to get from her. "Well, I've got some work to do. I need to talk with both of them to get a fuller picture of what was going on. After I do that, I'll want to talk to you about what I found out and where we go next. Does that make sense?" Joe asked.

She paused and looked at the floor before speaking softly. "I know you have to go through the motions and protect your teachers from moms like me who get labeled bitches in the teacher's lounge, but this mama bear's not gonna have Petersen or anybody mistreating my son. He's not a jock and that's what gets respect around here. Now he's got a stomachache all the time and says he hates school. And this is an A/B student! Or used to be!"

"Mrs. Rolling," Joe began.

"Janelle's fine," she interrupted.

"I've got a freshman son, too. Elliott. I know how important *and stressful* the freshman year can be. Nobody's going to label anyone—kid, parent, principal—well, maybe the principal," he said, trying to lighten things. "We want every student to like school, feel welcome, and experience success. I'm sorry that it seems like that has not happened in PE. I need to follow up and I'll be back in touch as soon as I've had a chance to do that," Joe said.

Realizing that the bell was about to ring, Joe tried to extend the conversation and engage in some small talk with Mrs. Rolling. He also wanted to let the bell ring so she wasn't thrown into the crowded hallway during passing time. He knew some parents found that uncomfortable, to say nothing of the way many high school kids felt about having a parent in the building. Either way, he felt it best to let the passing period end before sending Janelle on her way.

QUESTIONS

1. Joe has made defining "the Pinicon Way" a priority. Is this worth the time? What might come of the effort?
2. Evaluate Joe's meeting with Susan Shottenkirk. How should he proceed?
3. Sutt and Kristi have different ideas for dealing with Mace Stallworth. What should happen?
4. What is your position on a "no-zeros" grading policy? How should Kristi proceed?
5. Did Joe give Kristi good advice on handling "the Recess Quarterback"?
6. Evaluate Joe's actions related to the Confederate flag sale.

Chapter Twelve

Late October

Stepping Forward, Stepping Back, Staying Even?

A NICE PROBLEM TO HAVE

"We've never had something like this before," Mark Watters said. "The chance to spend some serious money for professional learning *and the opportunity to decide* how to spend it. I have to say thank you, Joe." The rest of the leadership team nodded in agreement.

The week before, Zylstra had told Joe she planned to include Pinicon staff on a professional learning initiative that Kessler was undertaking. McHale said the Kessler plans looked good, but suggested Joe might have an opportunity to score points with Pinicon staff by allowing them some freedom of choice. Joe took his advice and asked Zylstra if she would be willing to give Pinicon its share of the money to use as staff saw fit. Zylstra resisted initially, citing the goal of more sharing between the two campuses. She relented when Joe convinced her that shared decision-making and deferring to a leadership team was a new concept for Pinicon.

"Thanks, Mark," Joe said. "I'm happy that Dr. Zylstra is giving us this autonomy, because it's really important for us to have full ownership of our professional learning. I'd like you and the leadership team to take a look at the options and see what you think makes the most sense. My only request is that you tie your choice to our efforts to define the Pinicon Way."

With that, he left the leadership team to sort through ideas for how to allocate the funds.

TRAVIS'S SIDE

Joe's calendar listed minor (and some major) issues that he liked to call "Follow-up and Follow-through." He tried to complete at least five of them each day. Among them was talking with Travis Rolling to get his side of the story from Stu Petersen's PE class. Travis entered Joe's office wearing eye liner, baggy black jeans, a black and silver T-shirt with an elaborate design, and scrunched hair. A chain dangled from his belt loop into his pocket. He looked to Joe like an effeminate freshman who was outside the margins, looking for his niche.

"What caused you and Mr. Petersen to have some kind of problem?" Joe asked.

Travis said the class was in the gym waiting to be dismissed when he pointed out that several football players were sitting beneath Petersen's sign prohibiting sitting on the bleachers when in the closed position. "I asked him if he was going to get them off the bleachers and he freaked. He totally went off, like blew a gasket or something. You could see all the veins in his neck and stuff and he was screaming at me . . . something about 'I eat punks like you for lunch.' And I'm like, 'whatever,' I think I'll go sit on the bleachers so you don't *eat me.*"

Joe pictured Sutt bursting out in laughter at the way Travis told the story.

Joe asked, "Was there a problem earlier in the class? Or earlier this year?"

"Nope. I mean, he never even talks to me, because I'm not in football. He hates anyone who's not in football. And everyone tells me I need to be tougher, and I was kind of bawling about it, but mostly to see if it would make him feel bad. I really think he gets off on it."

"On what?" Joe asked.

"Ripping kids he hates," Travis said, matter-of-factly.

Joe began, "Well Travis, I appreciate you telling me what went on. I need to talk to Mr. Petersen too. How have things gone since that day?"

"Fine, I mean, the tears were an act mostly. I can cry right now if you want me to. I just think he should enforce his five thousand rules on everybody and not just the freaks like me."

"Nobody thinks you're a freak, Travis."

"You have to say that. Of course they do. But I'm good with it. It fits me."

Travis was right. Joe probably did have to say it. And it did seem that Travis embraced the label.

"Hey, I want you to enjoy school and do well. I want to help with that. Your teachers do too. If things have been working lately, keep doing what you're doing. And if you're having a hard time with kids or teachers, I want to know," Joe said.

"Yep," said Travis. "Can I go now?"

IS THAT RELEVANT?

Grandmotherly Joyce Barry had taught at Kessler High School for thirty-nine years and looked like someone cast to play a family and consumer science (FCS) teacher in a movie. Friendly though she was, connecting with students, particularly those who were required to take introductory FCS classes, didn't come easily for her. Nor did her new shared schedule, which required her to travel between the Kessler and Pinicon schools.

As had been the case with Patrazzo, the idea of a pre-observation confer-ence perplexed her. "You have the lesson plan. Why don't you just come see for yourself what we're doing?"

Joe said he wanted to know the background on the lesson and larger unit, which consisted of students making decorative pillows. When they finally found time to meet, Joyce talked at length about the process leading up to students starting to sew, which included measuring, fabric selection, reading patterns, different types of stitches, and maintenance of the sewing machine.

Joe was surprised to see that her lesson plans were printed on ancient-looking purple mimeographed paper, along with several worksheets and crossword puzzles about parts of the sewing machine, types of fabric, and other terms. She answered Joe's gentle question about staying current by naming Pinicon students who had gone on to study textile or culinary arts.

"That's great to hear," Joe said. "Have you been able to keep them en-gaged making pillows? You've clearly had success, but I couldn't help notic-ing that your plans and the worksheets look pretty old. I wonder if there is another project or way to engage the students."

He knew he had hit a nerve. "Mr. Gentry, I've had nearly four decades of success as a teacher in this field. And I can't remember being subjected to this kind of grilling, even before seeing me teach. I feel like I'm being interrogated at a trial."

"Oh, Joyce, I don't want you to feel that way at all. I'm just trying to get a feel for things before I observe. I was a social studies teacher, so I know showing relevance is not always easy."

On the day of the observation, Joyce had reserved a sewing machine and material for his use. He thanked her, but said he needed to observe and take notes and suggested that he might participate with the class another time. A couple of students flew through the lesson, but many struggled with their machines and measuring fabric. Others were without a clue. Joe was bothered that she never made contact with the strugglers.

In the post-observation conference, she lamented that students were less respectful and attentive than in the past. "Some of the gals show great promise. Others, like that scary Rolling boy dressed all in black, are just frightening."

Joe suggested that she should feel good that her students were not all girls. "I wonder if there are some ways we can work together to reach some of those who are struggling or not paying attention," Joe offered.

"I need to help the gals who are really trying. The others, like Trevor Rolling, would be better suited in shop or in a special program," she said.

"Well, the beauty is that everyone can take electives like yours. And it's *Travis* Rolling."

After that, Joyce shut down and said almost nothing for the rest of the meeting.

Two days later, he found a four-page, handwritten letter from Joyce addressed to Dr. Zylstra and the school board president in his mailbox. She said she had never felt so disrespected and bullied by an administrator. "Throughout this process, the quality and relevance of my teaching were thoroughly attacked and belittled; however, Mr. Joseph Gentry declined to participate in the lesson, even after I made special arrangements for him to do so, by providing a machine and the necessary materials. He clearly does not know the first thing about sewing, nor does he respect home economics, yet he attacked my lesson as irrelevant in today's world and accused me of being sexist against boys who are failing the class because of a lack of effort."

Kessler High principal Cal Murphy snickered when Joe asked about her performance there. "Before we go there, I think you need to show her that you know how to thread the bobbin and make a proper pillow. And I'll make a confession. I'm putting a student teacher in there next semester. I guarantee the quality of instruction will increase. She really needs to go."

When Joe recited Joyce's memo to McHale, he laughed for several seconds. "I agree with Murphy and love your enthusiasm, but your time might be better spent elsewhere. It's allocation of resources. Where can you make the most impact with the time you have?" McHale asked.

Ineffective as she was, Joe wondered if he had the heart to nudge Joyce to the door.

I'LL KNOCK 'EM OUT!

Richard Smith was a freshman transfer from Kessler with a lot of personality. His file indicated a few run-ins the year before, mostly for fighting and "insubordination," a term Joe found especially loaded and problematic, because it could mean just about anything, from being completely out of control to pushing back against a dictatorial teacher. He found it curious that Richard's time at Pinicon had been relatively uneventful, save for a few office referrals for profanity. Joe felt some teachers had extra-sensitive ears when it came to certain students.

He heard Richard coming toward his office before he saw him. He was unusually loud and visibly upset. He wailed, "I'm not gonna play that shit," slapping a stack of rectangular stickers down on Joe's desk.

"Hold up, Richard, hold up. What have you got?"

Joe slid some papers out of the way while Richard mumbled and paced in front of the desk. The stickers were Confederate flags about five inches long with "Pirate Pride" printed across them in gold letters.

For the next ten minutes, Joe had a hard time keeping Richard focused on where he had found the stickers, rather than what he said he would do to the person responsible. A couple had been hung on his and other African American kids' lockers. The rest were scattered around the building. "Show me where they were. Let's go," he said, leading Richard out of the office.

Richard seemed to enjoy walking the building to point out where he had found the stickers, and Joe thanked him for letting him know immediately. Then he tried a gamble. "I'm gonna need your help."

"What?" Richard asked, more calm but seeming suspicious.

"I need you to not say a word about this. Not to anybody, okay?"

Richard squinted.

"Because if you do, it's gonna make finding out who hung these up a lot harder. For right now, I need to keep this just between us while I look at the video cameras and investigate. You can really help me, but you have to keep it quiet. Will you do that?"

Being in on a secret seemed to appeal to Richard. Joe sent him back to class and made a quick call to Richard's mother, whom he had met in August when he visited new families at Kessler High. She appreciated the call and was glad that he was "aware of what's going on."

Joe pulled up the video from the interior hallway cameras, which showed only the Pepsi delivery man and Dave Crawford cleaning up lunch tables. He messaged teachers to immediately forward the names of anyone who was out of their sixth-period class for any amount of time. By the end of the hour, he had heard from everyone except Merle Richards and June Ramsey. He stopped in Ramsey's room on the way to Richards's shop.

He scanned the list to see if Cooper McDermott and Dan Arstman had signed out, having immediately suspected them, but then realized they had gone with Young to Manufacturing Day at the junior college. *Damn*, he said to himself. *I thought I had an easy one.*

Afternoon conversations with students who had signed out of classrooms produced no leads, nor did informal chats with Kessler transfer kids. Investigating took the rest of the day and caused him to miss a conference call with Rhonda Prior and a couple of regional math consultants about textbook selection. Joe typed out another staff message marked "high priority and confidential" explaining the situation and asking them to share any ideas they might have.

Parts of the job frustrated him immensely. Even though student discipline had a way of taking over at times, dealing with routine fights and misbehavior didn't really bother him much. But unnecessary meanness and harassment ate at him. *I'm gonna* hammer *somebody on this one if I can catch them*, he said to himself.

FOLLOW-THROUGH WITH STU

Joe had intended to talk to Petersen soon after visiting with Travis Rolling and his mother, but hadn't gotten to it. Slow follow-up had seemed inexcusable as a teacher and in grad school. But as principal, routine things often took far too long, though he wasn't sure why.

When Joe entered Petersen's overstuffed PE office, he found him pecking at the computer with his index fingers while Sports Center blared in the background.

"Hey, Mr. Gentry!" Petersen barked. "How's everything with the head pirate?"

"I haven't been asked to walk the plank yet!" Clearing a place to sit on an old gray chair, Gentry noticed Petersen's fantasy football roster on the computer screen.

"We should get you in the league next year," Petersen said, pointing to the screen. "We have a lot of fun. Relieves stress."

"I appreciate it but don't know enough football, and you guys would take my money."

"We're pretty low key, really. Everybody throws a few bucks in and the winner gets the pot at the end of the year. Keeps the old football guys alive," Petersen said.

Joe explained that Travis Rolling's mother had been to see him and did his best to communicate the emotion she had shown in his office. Petersen acknowledged that he had talked with her before about Travis's older siblings. "The Rollings are not in my fan club."

Joe was surprised that Petersen's account of the events was not much different from Janelle's. He acknowledged that he "got on him pretty good" and said that he'd seen a steady decline in the respect given to teachers and that Travis Rolling was a prime example.

"You've got kids who fly off at the mouth and expect the adults to tolerate it. Well, they know that doesn't work with me. Sometimes they need a reminder."

Joe related Travis's story about kids sitting on the bleachers and that Petersen got upset with him when he pointed it out. "Travis and his mother seem to think that you favor the athletes in class. That's not my view, Stu; I'm just telling you what we talked about. Was Travis crying while you were yelling at him?" Joe asked.

"Yeah, but he's kind of a puss."

"Travis said you have a lot of rules for PE."

"Absolutely. It's like Merle's accident in the shop. If someone is screwing around in the gym, someone will get hurt. So I run it pretty tight," Petersen said.

"Travis said you got upset when he pointed out that kids were sitting on the bleachers."

"Sure did. Anyone would have with his smartass tone. I don't need a kid pointing out what I can plainly see. And I got them off the bleachers in short order. I'm sure you've figured out that kids are going to test you, so we need clear rules. The way I handled Travis set the tone for being respectful and following simple rules they ought to be able to read."

"You bet. No question that kids—people—are going to test things at first," Joe said, hoping Petersen would catch the implication that he knew teachers would also test the principal. "Could the whole thing have been avoided by just telling the kids to get off the bleachers and talking to Travis privately about his tone of voice? Those battles with an audience of kids never end well. I'm wondering if that would have kept a kid from feeling like you hate him, a mom out of my office, and me out of yours," Joe commented, spinning an old football in his hands.

Petersen paused and studied Joe's face before speaking. "Joe, maybe I was a little loud with Rolling, but I'm not going soft on respect. Once you let up, it's over."

"I hear you. It's clear that Travis and his mom think you don't respect him because he isn't an athlete. And he *is* a different kid. Understand, I'm not saying you *don't* respect him. I'm saying their *perception is* that you don't. And if that's what they believe, well . . ."

Petersen cut him off. "I've dealt with all kinds in my years here. Discipline has slipped in the last couple. If you've got problems with my way of maintaining discipline, we ought to talk about that specifically and I'd appreciate having representation present."

"Understood, Stu," Joe said, surprised at Petersen's tone of voice and hostility. "I don't think it had to be that way. It shouldn't have escalated. And referring to him as a puss is unprofessional and unnecessary, even just between us. That said, I don't want to make a big deal out of this. I'm trying to help all sides here and get on with things."

"Doesn't feel like it to me, Joe," Petersen said, turning to his computer.

"I'd be happy to talk with you some more about it, and I'd welcome your union representative," Joe said softly. "Meantime, I'd appreciate your using Pinicon computers during the day for school business, not fantasy football. Check the contract."

As he left Petersen's office, Joe shook his head. He had hoped to convince Petersen to call Mrs. Rolling, talk to Travis, and defuse things, but the opposite had happened. Had he made a trivial matter worse? Or was a teacher bringing a freshman student to tears really trivial?

He had been trying to be more assertive at the right times and worry less about always being diplomatic. That was part of the reason for carrying the buckeye in his pocket. Elton Rash and Professor Summers gave it to people straight. Joe was sure the issues he was addressing needed attention, but wasn't sure if he was shooting straight or burning bridges.

TRAFFIC COP

Dave Crawford rarely complained. Today was an exception. He had been working on a broken pipe that had spewed water into Charity Hampton's music room on and off for a couple of days. Every time he thought he was finished, a new leak popped up, causing more damage to walls and ceiling tiles and ruining an expensive keyboard.

"I've got the Pepsi man and the bread guy out here for deliveries and they can't get in because these damn kids don't know how to park!" he growled over the radio. Joe knew an unhappy custodian makes an unhappy building, so he dropped Fullan's (2008) *What's Worth Fighting For in the Principalship* and headed out to the parking lot. Joe and Carrie ran down the drivers of the problem vehicles and got them moved, and Joe apologized to the Pepsi and bread men.

To Joe's dismay, the students' parking the next morning was equally problematic, this time impacting the milk delivery. That afternoon, Joe stood in the rain directing traffic as the students left. Once the parking lot was clear, he counted the available student spaces and made a note to ask Young's computer design class to make a plan to streamline the mess. Between students sent to the office, two substitute teachers who didn't show up, and a phone call from a state legislator who wanted information about the sharing arrangement with Kessler, Joe's schedule had blown up. *I make decent money, but I'm an expensive traffic cop*, he mused.

QUESTIONS

1. Should Joe give faculty some direction in determining professional-learning priorities or leave it up to them?
2. How should Joe proceed with what he heard from Janelle and Travis Rolling?
3. Evaluate Joe's interaction with Joyce Barry.
4. How effective was Joe's handling of the situation with Richard Smith?
5. Evaluate Joe's conversation with Stu Petersen.
6. Is it appropriate for Joe to spend time dealing with the parking lot or should that be handled by someone else?

Chapter Thirteen

Homecoming

Black, White, and Gray

HARRIED

Professor Summers liked to play both sides of issues and keep students guessing as to what he really thought. Thus, he had once lured Joe and his classmates into a debate about whether venerable high school traditions like homecoming and prom should be abandoned. Some had argued they were outdated, divisive popularity contests. Others saw them as community events that enhanced the school's overall mission and fostered school pride. One person said the conversation was pointless because "homecoming and prom are not going anywhere and no principal is going to kill them and keep his or her job." The hypothetical debate had been interesting, but it was only a memory now, as homecoming had arrived in Pinicon.

Based on discussion in the leadership team and advice from Jeralyn and McHale, Joe met with nearly a dozen school and community groups, including student council, the captains of the fall sports teams, and booster clubs. He wanted everyone to feel ownership in homecoming, from the planned festivities to behavioral expectations, as several teachers had complained that parts of homecoming the year before had gotten out of hand.

Despite the guidelines he had given the student council for dress-up days, Joe vetoed toga day, gender bender day, and horror movie day in favor of more benign themes. He had also put the kibosh on the powder puff football game, which still involved high school girls "playing football" while the football boys "coached." When students and several parents complained, he told them powder puff was a fine thing for their own time and off of school grounds.

When Joe arrived at school at 6:00 a.m. Monday, an unhappy sight greeted him. Nearly all the windows had been painted with bars to resemble a jail with "Fucking Fun Hater Gentry" painted across the glass doors at the main student entrance.

"You don't strike me as a fun hater," he heard Dave Crawford say from behind him. "I've got the other side of the building already cleaned off. I decided to leave that part for you to see," he snickered. "And I didn't know we had so many kids interested in med school."

"Med school?"

"They've got some pretty good drawings of male body parts," Crawford said, gesturing toward a couple of windows Joe hadn't noticed.

"Anything broken?" Joe asked.

"Nothing that I can see."

Joe snapped a picture of his monument to share with Sutt and Kristi and started scrubbing windows alongside Crawford. In an hour, they had most of the windows washed clean, with the help of some other custodians and an early morning detention student. At 9:15, he took a phone call from Don Mitchell, who said that "catching the little shits" should be his top priority. Joe told Mitchell that he had already spoken to Lieutenant Beckworth and the Pinicon police about increasing patrols for the week and investigating the mischief.

PIRATE PRODUCTION

Pinicon homecoming tradition included a different assembly or activity for the last forty minutes of each day of the week. The first day blew him away. Students from kindergarten through twelfth grade roared their approval at a slick video production that touted the academic and activities achievements of Pinicon students, along with short interview clips from parents, students, and community members. "This is like a college recruiting film," he told Young over the din of energy in the gym. Young explained that the video was an annual production by a Pinicon graduate who worked at a Kessler advertising agency. "We ought to get some kids up there for internship experiences or something," he told Young.

Following the video, student council president Becky Marks stepped to the microphone. "Better pay attention," Young told Joe with a nudge. Becky explained that on the Monday of homecoming week, tradition dictated that new Pinicon staff members participate in some friendly competition. "We have a new principal this year, Mr. Gentry. Come on down! You're a contestant in the Pinicon Olympics."

Joe found himself seated on a folding chair, facing the bleachers alongside Allison Jesup, Mark Watters, Rhonda Prior, and Gregg Altman. In front of each was a large bowl of fruit. A cheerleader explained that the five contestants were going to compete in the healthy eating contest. The person who ate the most fruit in the shortest amount of time would win a $50 gift card to the Pirate's Den Steakhouse.

The student body was on its feet chanting, "Altman, Altman," who encouraged their enthusiasm. Mark Watters stood and flexed his muscles in several different poses. Young, Jeralyn, and Carrie all shouted to Joe to make a good showing as the leader of the building. The cheerleaders blindfolded each contestant, reviewed the rules, and sounded the scoreboard buzzer to start the clock.

Joe started eating as music pumped through the gym. Familiar and unfamiliar voices began screaming at him to go faster as cheerleaders handed him cut pineapples, orange slices, grapes, and peeled bananas. Fruit tumbled out of his mouth and onto his lap and the floor.

As the buzzer sounded to stop the competition, the roar of the students was deafening. When the cheerleaders removed his blindfold, Joe saw Jeralyn, Allison, Watters, Altman, and Prior and a student with a small video camera directly in front of him. All were laughing hysterically. When Joe realized he had been the only one eating, he threw the remains of a banana at Prior and Watters, prompting even more reaction from the crowd.

The student council president announced that the winner would be determined by a video replay. The Shottenkirk Tire & Appliance Video Screen came to life with a slow-motion video of Joe stuffing himself while the other "contestants" removed their blindfolds and moved their chairs to watch him make a fool of himself. Joe laughed so hard, he was sweating. The rest of the assembly was a blur, with students and teachers slapping his back like he was some kind of hero. Did it make a difference if they were laughing at him or with him?

BUSINESS AS UNUSUAL

Joe made his customary rounds during homecoming week and was pleased that most teachers and students were making a reasonable effort to get something accomplished. Claire reminded him how much they had enjoyed homecoming in high school when he grumbled about the disruption.

"Maybe that kid who painted 'Fun Hater' was right?" she teased.

"It's not like anyone comes *home* for it. It's not an alumni event," he said.

"Of course not, but if you can't have some fun in high school, when can you? Loosen up, Mr. Principal." She forced Joe to make good on her suggestion when she and Margaret presented him with a thrift-store pirate suit. Elliott just shook his head and laughed. Plus, after Monday afternoon's Healthy Eating Contest, what did he have to lose? He felt like he had a shot to win the faculty/staff division of the Pirate Look-Alike Contest.

THE VOTES ARE IN

Joe had finished telling a couple of dozen students who had stretched pirate day to include pimps and naughty nurses to change their clothes when Jeralyn brought in the king and queen ballots. As they poured the ballots onto the table in his office, she noted how well the week had gone, save for Monday's minor vandalism, which was still unsolved. "I think you did a great job of keeping it fun but increasing the focus on academics, too. Dedicating one of the assemblies to academics, arts, and service and getting the paper to cover it was a great idea. It has been nice to shine some light on those. Thanks for that," she said.

"You're just hoping I forget your role in the fruit hazing incident," he teased.

"I've dealt with tougher customers than you," she countered. He knew she was right.

As they counted the ballots, Derrik Dempsey, the youngest of three boys who lived with their outlaw father, began piling up votes. Derrik's mother had left several years before, unwilling to endure more verbal and physical abuse from her husband.

The Pinicon staff had informally decided that the best way to deal with the family was to keep the father as far from the building as possible, lest he show up drunk or high and make a scene. Although Derrik could be a pain, he was mostly a reckless daredevil and comedian. The abhorrent treatment of women he had learned from his father produced trouble with just about every staff member except Jeralyn. For whatever reason, the family usually got on with her fairly well. Jeralyn's count concluded that Derrik received four more votes than his nearest rival—an honor student, athlete, and member of the National Honor Society.

"I was afraid this might happen," Jeralyn sighed. "Derrik's made a mockery of just about everything around here and now they want him for king. He got busted for pot last spring, and I told Jerry Hughes we needed a policy change to prevent this, but he was already mentally retired and didn't do anything."

"I've dealt with him a few times and suspended him once. That disqualifies him."

"It *should*, but right now it's not in the policy. We begged Jerry to update it but he didn't. The hell of it is that Derrik is smart enough to know that."

"This is why I hate homecoming. Well, *hate* is too strong, but there's so much wrong with this picture," Joe said. "Let's count the girls."

Shelby Gibson, who Jeralyn described as an absolute joy, received the most queen votes.

"She must be," said Joe flatly, "because I don't even know her."

Jeralyn popped open a Cherry Coke. "There's your Pinicon royalty, Joe. King of the Losers and the Queen of Hearts. The results have been certified and verified."

"Or have they?" asked Joe.

Jeralyn looked at Joe quizzically.

"I think we should recount them. We want to get it right. These are some pretty high stakes," Joe said, lips pursed. "If we're committed to doing what is best for kids and the school, that doesn't include allowing them to make a joke of things. Or embolden an idiot kid."

Jeralyn paused again, understanding the implication. "How does that square with respect, responsibility, honesty, and courtesy, Joe?"

"I *respect* the Pinicon kids and school and it's my *responsibility* to protect the school environment. I'm *honestly* committed to doing what's best. That includes who gets the homecoming spotlight. As for *courtesy*, I'm a nice guy."

Jeralyn didn't speak for several minutes while Joe recounted the king ballots.

"After recounting, Derrik finished second. Do you want to count them again yourself?"

"No, maybe a couple of ballots were stuck together the first time," she said tentatively.

"You're sure you can live with this result, Jeralyn?"

"It's a little awkward, but you're the principal."

FATHER, WE ASK YOUR GUIDANCE . . .

Tossing the football around before supper, Joe asked Elliott if he regretted his decision not to play football, given that Pinicon was so football crazy and Larry Den Herder so admired.

"Not really," said Elliott, lofting the ball across the yard. "It's just not my thing."

"I'm glad you're comfortable. And you have plenty of time to change your mind."

"It's funny how football is everything here. They take it *so* seriously," Elliott observed.

"Sure do," Joe agreed. "It's almost like football is the religion, like *Friday Night Lights.*"

"Pretty much is, with the prayer and everything."

Joe caught the ball and cocked his head at Elliott. "*Prayer* and everything?"

"Yeah. The pregame prayer. Coach prays to keep everybody safe and thanks God for health and opportunity to play and stuff, not to win the game or anything," Elliott said.

"Coach *leads* the prayer?"

"Yep."

Perfect, Joe thought. *Just in time for homecoming.*

The next morning, after his walk through Richards's shop, Joe caught Young at his desk and asked him if he knew about the prayer.

"Yep. Done it for as long as I can remember. The man is strong in his faith."

"A lot stronger in his faith than his knowledge of the law," Joe said, dropping into Young's worn La-Z-Boy.

"Yeah, never been an issue, though. People have so much respect for Larry; it's hard for them to separate the coach from what he's done in church and the community. And he's made a helluva difference in a lot of kids' lives."

"But you know it's illegal, right?"

"Sure I do. Talked with Jerry Hughes about it a few years ago. Let a sleeping dog lie was Jerry's position and I agree. It's not hurting anybody and there's nothing to gain by bringing it up. You see it differently?"

"I'm not into knowingly running over kids' rights if I can help it."

"Good thing Juneau Hall doesn't know the Constitution like you do," Young laughed. "You ran over his on the first day of school when you kicked him out of the gym."

"That I did. And shouldn't have, but Don Mitchell didn't leave me much choice."

"I guess not. But you have a choice here and there's nothing to gain. No one's objected. The team's doing well."

Joe sighed. "I was just playing a nice game of catch with my son and now this."

"Oh, hell. You mean *Elliott's* the one who told you and not some parent from the ACLU?" Young laughed. "He's the informant?"

Joe nodded and said that he and Claire had worried about the difficulties of being the principal's kid in high school, choosing not to play football at a place like Pinicon, "and just about everything else parents can worry about. I don't want an informant. I just want to be able to talk to my son. And this time, he told me something I kind of wish he wouldn't have."

"Yeah, chief. I'm sure it's tough being the principal's kid, but it's a non-issue. Larry's not *imposing* his religion on the kids. It's giving thanks and asking for safety. Nothing wrong with that. You'll have plenty of bigger fish to fry," Young said as the bell rang.

PINICON ROYALTY

The gym was packed with students, parents, and even some alumni for the coronation of the homecoming king and queen. As he prepared to announce the king and queen, Joe wondered if the results would be controversial. He remembered how Professor Summers had insisted that "the thing that rises up to bite you is rarely the thing you're anticipating." He had told Mitchell that he and Lieutenant Beckworth had no real leads on the vandalism but the rest of the week had been uneventful. Despite that, Mitchell said he wanted Joe to lean harder on the kids and suggested Joe threaten to cancel the dance unless the culprits came forward.

Young and McHale disagreed, insisting that Mitchell's suggestion was an overreaction. "Tell Mitchell that you warned students that homecoming might look a lot different if the pranks continued and that took care of it. That's responding and it also lets you be more or less honest with Mitchell, who always wants to be Rambo," McHale advised. Joe took the advice and hoped Mitchell wouldn't push any harder.

Joe strode to the podium with an envelope in his suit pocket. "It is my pleasure to introduce this year's Pinicon Homecoming Court," he said, reading a short paragraph about each candidate as they walked to a spot behind him. He wondered if it would seem awkward that all of the candidates except Derrik Dempsey had extensive involvement in school, church, and community activities. Reading Dempsey's painfully short resume felt odd to Joe, but the crowd seemed not to notice.

Joe opened the envelope as the band struck a drum roll. "Please welcome this year's Pinicon homecoming king and queen, Mr. Mike Vawter and Miss Shelby Gibson!" Joe said as the band struck up "On Pinicon." Jeralyn placed an awkward-looking crown and tiara on each as photos snapped.

Next and perfectly on cue, Tony Morsorano, the lone senior on the cross-country team, burst through the gym doors, dressed in his blue and gold uniform and carrying the game ball, which the cross-country team had ceremonially carried for sixty-seven miles—one for each member of the football team. Morsorano handed the ball to Den Herder, who gestured him to the podium.

Morsorano, who had a cool, confident manner, said it was an honor to continue the tradition of presenting the game ball and wished the football team good luck. Joe was pleased that he praised the fall sports teams, coaches, band, and teachers. He said that seniors' time was running short and encouraged everyone to get involved in school activities, whether clubs, the arts, or sports. "Get involved, even if it's just cross country, because it beats doing nothing and sitting around smoking pot," he said, looking over his shoulder, squarely at Derrik Dempsey.

With roughly a third of the crowd laughing, another third roaring, and a final third gasping, Joe took the microphone. There was Professor Summers's unexpected biter. Joe thanked the student council, band, cheerleaders, and the students for their enthusiasm and wished the team good luck and encouraged all to have a safe, fun-filled weekend. "And Tony, I need to see you in my office. Right now," Joe said, as pleasantly as he could manage.

SKYPE CONFERENCE

Joe shared the story of the homecoming ballots. Kristi spoke first, arguing that Joe's experience proved that the whole thing should be re-envisioned to be something more than a 1950s popularity contest. "But I don't think the recount was a good move, Joe. What are you gonna do when all the kids say they voted for the renegade?"

"I just couldn't let it happen. Derrik Dempsey is the *poster child* for someone who should never be homecoming king. And I guarantee I'll get the policy changed for next year. You think I was unethical?"

"I'm just saying I couldn't have done it," Kristi said.

"I might have let him win and tried to make it a learning opportunity," Sutt said. "But maybe that's easy for me to say."

They debated Joe's actions for a few more minutes before Joe brought up the pregame prayer. "You have no choice but to act on it," Kristi began. "I know the coach is a great guy, but that doesn't change the fact that it's against the law."

Sutt countered that there was nothing to be gained by alienating Den Herder. "Hell, Joe, the guy is *Mr. Pinicon* and has been in your corner so far. Why call him out on something positive that he's been doing forever? When the Pirate fans hear that the rookie principal is battling him over this, they're gonna go ape shit. I wouldn't touch that with a stick!"

"So a legendary coach and a good team mean we ignore the law?" Joe asked.

"Make it so the kids do the prayer on their own. Otherwise you're starting an unnecessary fight," Sutt said. "Classic case of following the law but hurting yourself in the process. You know everyone in that town thinks it's great. Let it ride unless the ACLU calls."

Joe turned the conversation to Elliott. "What about my son?" he asked.

"Be glad he's not playing football and getting his constitutional rights trampled," Sutt laughed.

"Good one, smart ass. If I do nothing, what does that tell him? That all the stuff I've tried to teach him about doing the right thing was just talk? Do as I say and not as I do?"

"*Oooh*," Kristi said. "I don't have kids and hadn't thought about that. Yuck."

"It's a lesson in practicality," Sutt interjected. "The law is the law, but you also gotta use common sense. If you're gonna deal with it, wait until June. The timing is all wrong, man."

"I hear you, Sutt," Kristi said, "but Joe's selling out if he doesn't do anything. What kind of lesson is that for Elliott?"

Unable to come to agreement, Joe asked about the way he had handled Stu Petersen and Pat Patrazzo. "I have these unexpectedly tense conversations. Patrazzo was questioning my qualifications as an observer, blah, blah, blah, and I wound up telling him it was bullshit and he needed to be more professional. Then he used it against me."

"I think you handled Patrazzo fine. He's probably been left alone because no one wants to deal with him. You're probably the first one to stand up to him," Sutt said.

Kristi's view was less positive. "You can't let him push you around, and you were in good shape until you told him it was bullshit. You had the high road until that point."

"He was testing me and I let him win. Shit. What about Petersen? Did I wreck that too?"

"Hell no," Sutt said. "I love that you brought in the union rep and playing fantasy football on the school's computer. If he wants to talk contract, go for it! Plus, you stood up for the kid."

"I like that one too, Joe. Sounds like he was mistreating a kid, so he gets what he gets. The difference is that you didn't get pulled into the language. You were playing tit for tat, but I think it's okay for people to see the principal get mad. Shows we're human. Maybe they respect you for standing up to them, but of course they'll never admit it."

Kristi shared a triangular relationship between a student teacher and two Winthrop teachers. Rumor held that a married female teacher in her fifties had become involved with a new male teacher, also married. Things boiled over when a female student teacher in her early twenties assigned to the older female teacher started spending a lot of time in the younger male teacher's room.

"The student teaching supervisor gave me four pages of emails between the teachers. They're calling each other everything in the book like mean high school girls going at it."

"All of this done on school email? During school?" Sutt asked.

"Oh yeah," said Kristi.

"That is one your superintendent is gonna want to know about," Joe said.

"I say bring 'em in and have them read the really bad stuff back to you," Sutt suggested. "Then ask what the hell their students are doing during their little pissing match."

"Too late. I brought them to my office and read some of it back to them and said their email has been disabled until they want to act like adults. Then I said I had to leave and left them sitting there together. Maybe a little heavy handed, but seriously, grow up." Kristi laughed.

"We've dominated the discussion, Sutt. What's up with you?" Joe asked.

"Another couple of weeks in paradise," Sutt said. "We had a teacher fire his shotgun in the air when some kids showed up to TP his house for homecoming. Made the news and everything. Freaking lunatic. We suspended him for five days and I think Rudy is going to tell him to resign or the board is coming after him."

Sutt said he had spent about twenty hours interviewing students who witnessed the shotgun blast and looking at school bus video trying to determine the source of two empty beer cans found on a field trip bus. "All those hours for a couple of empty cans of Flatlander Light. I did get myself in another little mess, though. Total bullshit."

"Do tell," prompted Kristi.

"You remember me telling you about the O'Malleys? They have a special-needs freshman, Grace. Sweet girl. Uses a walker. I got off to a horrible start with them."

Sutt had promised to arrange for someone to help Grace find her classes on her first days of school. "I had it all set up with a student council girl, but she was sick on Grace's first day. Nobody checked on her, and she got lost. Total mess. Mom was pissed and came in here and lit me up. I couldn't blame her and promised we would do better."

"I like that you admitted the mistake," Kristi said. "Did it help?"

"A little. Mom told me the freshman girl's bathroom stall was too narrow for Grace's walker. So she had to use one at the other end of the school. I filled out the maintenance request, and those SOBs had three weeks to do it and nothing happened. Now I look like a total loser. So mom called last week and went off again. I told her I had asked maintenance to fix it and they hadn't gotten it done yet. She said it was inexcusable. And I agreed with her. So, that weekend, I fixed the damn stall myself, and I called and told her so."

"That's pretty cool, Sutt. I like it," said Joe. "She had to see that you are trying."

"I think so. I have been checking on Grace every day, and man, she is a fun kid. But the other day I get a grievance from the director of maintenance for infringing on his guys' job!"

"Get out!" Kristi shrieked.

"I kind of went off. I shouldn't have, but it felt good. I said if his guys would get off their asses, I wouldn't have had to fix it myself. And of course, the maintenance guy called the superintendent, who called Rudy, who brought me into his office."

Sutt said the conversation with Rudy went well. "He had already called them to say there was no excuse for the delay and that it wasn't on me. He really supported me, though he did tell me to back off the maintenance guys a little."

"You're a bull in a china shop," Joe laughed.

"I've been on a roll. I challenged the other assistant principals in our conference to take the state Academic Progress Tests next semester. It made the newspaper. Rudy says he wants to use it to start a discussion about whether we have an *achievement gap* or a *test score gap*. I bombed some of those tests in high school, so I might embarrass us!"

"That's a good example of how instructional leadership is not just teaching teachers. It can be starting conversations," Kristi noted. "I'm going to ask my teachers to take some of the tests. We've got so much *data* and so little *information*. We do absolutely nothing with all this stuff we collect, but that's another story. Can I give you one more dilemma?"

"Only if it's easy," Joe said.

Kristi described a troubling classroom observation with a brand-new second-grade teacher. "I honestly think people off the street could have done a better job. I couldn't see any objectives; she was over their heads and couldn't tell they were lost. And she just kept going."

"Did you stop her?" Sutt asked.

"No. But I wonder if I should have. I mean, it was horrible, but I thought letting her struggle might be a teachable moment. And I thought intervening might strip her of her power and embarrass her. I can't decide if she is pretending things are going well or if she is just clueless. Should I have stepped in?"

"That's a hard one. I can see both sides," Joe said. And their debate began.

QUESTIONS

1. How much time should Joe allocate to investigating the homecoming mischief?
2. Associate Superintendent Mitchell pressed Joe to threaten to cancel the dance. McHale and Young advised him to put Mitchell off. Was that good advice?
3. Evaluate Joe's handling of the homecoming ballots.
4. What action, if any, should Joe take related to the football prayer?
5. Evaluate Kristi's handling of the two teachers' email feud.
6. Did Sutt act inappropriately with the Grace O'Malley restroom maintenance request?
7. Should Kristi have intervened during the teacher's ineffective lesson?

Chapter Fourteen

Early November

Fights, Fatigue, Poems, and Prayers

THE KITCHEN IS THE MOST DANGEROUS
ROOM IN THE HOUSE

Joyce Barry's operatic voice summoned Joe to a fight in the foods room. When he arrived, he saw spilled food, broken dishes, and wide-eyed students covered in what looked like ingredients for lasagna. Richard Smith, Sam Shottenkirk, and Javaris Hayes wore the most.

"These three have to go," Barry said, visibly shaken. Joe wondered how many fights had broken out in her foods classes during her long career. He supposed not many, as she had little idea of what had happened. Questioning them led to different accounts, but Joe concluded that Sam Shottenkirk had tried to put a Pinicon Pride Confederate flag sticker on Javaris Hayes's notebook while Hayes was putting cottage cheese into the lasagna pan. Smith saw this and confronted Shottenkirk, who shoved him away, spilling a couple of pans and starting the melee.

Joe had pieced most of the story together when Travis Rolling tapped on his office door and asked if he wanted to see a cell phone video of what happened. "I knew something was going to happen and I thought it would be cool to record it," Travis said. The video matched Joe's impression of what had happened. It showed Shottenkirk mumbling something to Smith, who exploded, tackling him and sending ingredients flying. The video showed

Hayes standing by with little or no involvement, other than dragging Smith off Shottenkirk, who denied everything until Joe played the video for him.

Joe suspended Smith and Shottenkirk for three days each. Smith's parents had little to say. Susan Shottenkirk was, as Joe anticipated, livid, saying his story must be true and noting that her son had never been suspended before. "Some dirtbag attacks my son for no reason and Sam gets suspended? This is not happening!" she protested.

She declined his invitation to take a look at the video. Joe also shared his suspicion that Sam was behind the stickers Smith had found around the building a few weeks prior. "That amounts to harassment. *Racially based* harassment, and that's a real problem," he said. "The fight is one thing. Involvement in the stickers is another."

Susan insisted that her son was not the aggressor and threw no punches. Joe wanted to say that was because Richard Smith kicked his ass. Instead, he chose his words carefully. "My interviews and the video suggest otherwise. I'm not condoning the other kid tackling him, but a lot of kids are going to react physically to that sort of thing. He can't be surprised."

It was the talk of the school for a couple of days. And Joe felt certain it wasn't finished.

RESTART

Time had gotten away from him, and the situation with Patrazzo continued to bother Joe. Stopping by Patrazzo's classroom, he asked about restarting their conversation, "in the spirit of détente," invoking Patrazzo's earlier reference. Patrazzo said he was fine with it.

Joe began by saying he loved the Boston Massacre topic. "Even though policymakers are obsessed with all the STEM stuff, social studies is more important than ever, because it's all about people and culture. That's pretty important in the world right now."

Patrazzo nodded in agreement. "I want informed people who will get a job, pay taxes, and support me in my retirement." His take was different than Joe's, but maybe they were getting somewhere. "I know you'd like to see me doing a bunch of group work and projects," Patrazzo said. "But that's not me. They get that elsewhere. Plus, in college, they're gonna sit in a lot of lectures. They're not gonna be asked to get in groups and make a collage about D-Day."

"Universities don't hold a monopoly on good teaching, that's for sure. Pat, you've got great knowledge of history. Much better than mine. And I don't think lecturing is all bad. I want to deal with content in an engaging, active way that builds teachers' and students' skills in communicating, writing, conducting research, using technology. I want everybody *thinking*."

"History is written by the victors," Patrazzo said.

"It sure is, and the vanquished would write it differently," Joe said. "That's what makes it so fascinating. That's one of the ideas I had about the Boston Massacre lesson. What if I presented it from the British point of view and we let students compare? I'm not the world's best social studies teacher, but would you be up for some team teaching? An experiment?" Joe asked.

Patrazzo said he would think about it.

GASSED

Joe didn't feel ill, but was tired in a different sort of way; it felt more permanent, not something a few lazy weekends would cure. He had survived homecoming, and Mitchell seemed to have forgotten that the vandalism culprits had not been caught. On the upside, his mentoring meetings with Tom McHale had exceeded his expectations and always left him more energized. He felt increasingly comfortable confiding in McHale, who was always talking about maintaining a life balance.

There was no single issue weighing Joe down. Babysitting Merle Richards was a headache; student discipline and parent issues seemed to come in waves. McHale and Murphy insisted that things were going well and that Joe's exhaustion was rooted in the sheer number of issues and the effort he was giving them, not an abundance of problems. "It's November of the first year. That's the nature of the job and it's easy to underestimate how constantly *being on* drags you down," McHale warned.

Few things occupied Joe's mind more than the prospect of telling Den Herder his pregame prayer had to end, especially with the team still alive in the state playoffs. He remembered Professor Summers saying that leaders usually know what they *need* to do, but only sometimes have the courage to do it. Like Young, McHale had known about the prayer for years and been content to let it slide. He worried Joe lacked sufficient credibility in the community to take it on. Conversely, Cal Murphy at Kessler said it was something he simply had to address. Joe's final call for advice had been to Professor Summers, who didn't answer.

Joe called Zylstra to tip her off about the prayer, looking for support and advice at the same time. "To be perfectly honest, I'm concerned about alienating Larry and getting killed in the community over this, especially with the team still playing, but don't feel I have a choice."

Zylstra sympathized with Joe's position. "Sometimes the superintendent can really help by playing the bad guy, which I don't mind doing. But in this case, I think you have to do it for credibility's sake, but I don't mind if you wait until the season is over. You have an obligation to protect the district—and the kids, though few will see it that way. It doesn't change any of the other great things he does for kids. This is just a little over the line."

Joe hung up the phone and leaned back in his chair. *Would it have been easier if Den Herder were a weak teacher? Or one who was not particularly supportive of him?* He wondered if he was too wrapped up in the politics and self-preservation.

IT'S UN-AMERICAN

The same afternoon, Joe took a call from Gene DeVore, the school board member and banker who had helped his family get settled in Pinicon. Joe admired DeVore's sunny disposition and boundless energy. He and Claire made sure DeVore knew how much they appreciated his help in landing her job at Walsh Furniture and Design in downtown Pinicon.

Joe liked being able to hear people talk in the outer office. It gave him a chance to prepare or sometimes discreetly close his door or pick up the phone if he wanted to be "unavailable." He rose to greet DeVore, who was teasing Carrie about coming to work at the bank—something he did every time he visited the school. "We pay better. *A lot* better," he joked.

"Gene, I've thrown people out of the building; don't make me do it to you," Joe said laughingly, shaking DeVore's hand. "And if she goes, I go," he added. "Come to think of it, there are some around here who would like to see *me* go," he said to laughter among all three. "Come on in."

Sitting in Joe's office, they exchanged small talk about Pinicon football and Claire's job. He wanted to know if Joe hunted. "Nope. They'd be safe with me out there. What brings you up, Gene?"

DeVore said he was visiting as a parent, rather than a school board member, and that he wanted to discuss something his daughter had shared from Allison Jesup's English class.

"Miss Jesup does a great job getting them thinking and that's not always easy," Joe said.

"What do you know about the poetry unit?" DeVore asked, sliding a few photocopied pages across the table.

Joe scanned the copies, some of which were student written. Others were copied from poetry books, journals, and magazines. Topics ranged from music to sexuality, war, disease, racism, parents, and sports. Some were light and benign. Others were darker.

"I don't know specifics, but I know she has had the kids looking at poetry and music as windows into culture. And a lot of it is social commentary—you know, writing about what is wrong with the world and that kind of thing."

"Do you think that's appropriate?"

"Social commentary and what's wrong with the world? Absolutely. Our kids see the news. I don't think we do high school kids any favors by shielding them from the harsh realities of life. But I also know that makes some people uncomfortable."

"Well, flip through some of those and I bet you'll change your mind. Keep in mind, these are written by our kids."

"I'm not much of a poet, but I like edgy stuff that makes me think. Or makes students think. I'd have to look through what's here to get a feel for it," Joe said.

"That sounds like a politician's answer," DeVore said, losing the sunny Pinicon Chamber of Commerce disposition.

Joe wasn't familiar with the Pinicon policy on controversial classroom materials but now wished that he was. He wanted to adequately support Allison Jesup, who was one of the most talented rookie teachers he'd seen. Her enthusiasm was contagious and her classroom was always lively. At the same time, he knew that local contexts held a lot of influence over what was seen as acceptable and what was out of bounds. And DeVore was a board member.

"Some of the political stuff . . . we've got parents defending the country while the school has kids read this crap? And then some Kessler kid writes soldiers are only there because they didn't have any other options."

"First of all, Gene, if they're here, they're *Pinicon* kids."

"Right. Well, Javaris Hayes wrote something about minorities and poor people always going off to fight in rich white people's wars. *F— the Chickenhawks* is the name of his poem."

"That's interesting. I've hardly heard him speak since he's been here."

"Joe, I think a lot of this is in poor taste, but I'm pretty conservative. And my opinion is probably beside the point. I don't want to meddle. Maybe I just needed to talk about it. I don't want it to be a problem for you, Miss Jesup, or anyone else."

"Gene, I really appreciate you letting me know. I hope I've explained myself. I'll talk with Miss Jesup about the project and how it fits into the curriculum. Can I get back with you?"

NO GO

Joe gave Young the option of being present when he talked to Coach Den Herder about the prayer. "It's probably appropriate that I'm there, even though I think we should let it go. But I'm a good soldier," Young said.

"I know we're not in total agreement, Frank. Everyone respects the coach and his faith. I'm just gonna tell him that him *leading* the prayer creates a legal liability for us that we can't have. If the kids want to pray, have a moment of silence, or whatever, that's all good. We aren't—I'm not—attacking anyone or his program. We're *protecting* it."

"You're the boss. Spin it that way if you want, but he won't see it that way. Let's just get it over with. This is why you get the big bucks," he snickered as Joe shot him a look.

Joe and Young met Den Herder in his classroom during his planning period. Joe said he didn't want to take a lot of Den Herder's time, given his limited planning time and the pressure of football playoffs. "The way you've handled the season speaks to your reputation. Even kids who have seen their playing time decrease haven't missed a beat. I wish our school could blend together as effectively as you have as a team."

"I appreciate that, Joe. We've got great guys and Kessler kids have added a lot. But I know that's not why you guys are here. What's up?"

Joe cut to the chase. "Coach, talk to us about the pregame prayer."

Den Herder said the prayer began spontaneously fifteen years earlier, when a member of the team had been seriously injured in a car accident. One of the players asked if the team could pray for their buddy, and it had become a part of the team's pregame routine since.

"What a great thing for the kids to start," Joe said. "The respect people have for you, your faith, and Pinicon football is inspiring. That said, we can't have *you* leading a locker room prayer with the kids."

Den Herder held Joe's gaze. After a few seconds, the coach broke the silence. "Joe, I don't pressure anyone to participate. Not one bit. They've *asked* me to do it. I've officiated at kids' funerals, prayed with kids about quitting drugs, to keep their parents together—you name it. I don't know who goes to church and who doesn't. It's quiet reflection time for some and a prayer for others and no one is singled out. It's just what we do."

"Larry, I don't *personally* have an issue with it. And I know it's something a lot of people expect. The issue is a legal one. I'm trying, we're trying to protect you, the team, and the district. That's all. Sometimes we can do things until we're called on it, and that's the case here. You can't *lead* the prayer. If the kids wanna do it on their own, that's fine. It just can't be you."

"So it's a problem *now*? After fifteen years? What else are we scrapping all of the sudden? This is *helping*, not hurting kids, Joe." Den Herder's famous fire was now visible in his eyes. The coach said little more, the silence lingering.

Joe said the conversation was not one he wanted to have but that he had no choice. "I hope it won't cause you to doubt the admiration that I have for you and your work at Pinicon." He tried in vain for a bit of small talk, but Den Herder was finished. Joe wished the team good luck in the playoffs and awkwardly walked out, hoping it was the end of the issue.

THE WATCH LIST

Jeralyn handed Joe the "Watch List," which consisted of an alphabetical listing of students she was "actively working with." To his surprise, it also included some faculty names. "I never break confidentiality with the kiddos, but you need to know what some of the issues are with my hip surgery coming up. Maybe keep an eye on them so they know your door is open. I doubt anyone will even notice I'm gone."

Joe hated to have Jeralyn gone from school, even for a few weeks. He realized that replacing a good counselor wasn't at all like bringing in a capable substitute teacher. Joe thanked her and looked over the list. "I guess one of the luxuries of our size is that we know most of the people and situations already." One name caught his eye. "What's up with Robin Stiles?"

Jeralyn had written the word "abyss" next to her name. Joe knew she had been working hard to convince Robin's parents of the seriousness of her mental-health problems. Though Jeralyn doubted they understood the severity of their daughter's issues, they had agreed to a two-week psychiatric commitment and evaluation at a hospital. "That might be one of my crowning achievements," she said. "You know Robin Stiles and Bill Kurowski are cousins, right? Both families are *really* private."

"What's the abyss?" Joe asked.

"On her bad days, that's what she says she's looking into. I hope it's gone well in the hospital. She's supposed to be back at school about the time I go to surgery. I hope to get her settled in, but keep an eye on her. File it away in that busy little head of yours, okay?"

"Okay. Are there teachers or kids she connects with? Friends?" Joe asked.

"Honestly, not really. She's so withdrawn. She'll be on some medication and will probably be pretty zonked. I don't want to make a bigger deal of it than it is. Just a heads-up."

After their meeting, Joe added a reminder to his blog for teachers about the importance of being available to students at all times, but especially during Jeralyn's upcoming absence.

SPIN CYCLE

Joe felt he had done a reasonably good job building relationships with the media in both Pinicon and Kessler. The bimonthly column Joe had volunteered to write for the *Pinicon Herald* provided a couple of well-written stories each month and was easy to produce, since it borrowed heavily from his blog. His tone was always positive, focusing on students, the good work of Pinicon faculty, and opportunities for community involvement. He dealt with Kessler TV, newspaper, and radio much less frequently, as Don Mitchell handled most of those requests and seemed to enjoy it.

Joe was judging student-created models in Rhonda Prior's geometry class when Homer Spurlin, the *Herald*'s jack-of-all-trades publisher, stopped by. When Joe called him back, he said he was preparing a story on the shared superintendent arrangement and asked about Joe's first few months at Pinicon. He enjoyed answering the questions, seizing on the opportunity to give what Professor Summers called "CMOT—a consistent message over time."

The headline a few days later was a surprise: "Locals: Kessler-Pinicon Partnership a Mixed Bag." To Joe's dismay, the article quoted heavily from well-known Pinicon residents who were critical or uninformed, including Susan Shottenkirk. She expressed concerns about "maintaining Pinicon's proud identity and traditions" in light of "changes like we've never seen."

Beyond a new principal, the presence of a few minority kids, and some shared teachers, he wondered what those might be. Others insinuated that student discipline had slipped, too.

That's code for a soft principal, less playing time, and some new minority and special-ed kids, Joe thought to himself.

He was not surprised to see board member and Pinicon promoter Gene DeVore quoted. No one could write about Pinicon without including De-Vore. "I think we're in a transition phase," DeVore said. "We have a lot of time-honored practices and traditions that seem to be changing. That can be hard. But this is still a great place with a bright future and a lot of pride."

Quotes from teachers were more balanced. Rhonda Prior said, "The shar-ing arrangement is an exciting opportunity for kids and teachers." Mark Watters saw great potential, but said, "The devil is in the details and we're working hard to make sense of it." Stu Petersen was quoted as saying, "It has taken a lot of time to assimilate new students and staff to the Pinicon Way."

There it was again. The ill-defined *Pinicon Way*. Joe seethed at the subtle jab he felt in Petersen's quote. He also objected to the word *assimilate,* taking it to mean that anyone new had to be shown the *right way* to do things. Petersen seemed about the last one qualified to judge. And it was clear who Petersen meant by "new staff." Was he being too sensitive?

It seemed that many locals saw a familiar Pinicon fading away. Joe's quotes were positive and well-polished, but sounded out of sync with the overall tone of the article, save for comments from Zylstra and Mitchell, which were upbeat but also differed from what the article presented as the prevailing view in Pinicon.

The only other positive came from "former Kessler football star turned Pinicon Pirate Javaris Hayes," who said, "Pinicon is more of a family type school than Kessler." Joe smiled at the quote, but still felt like the victim of a sneak attack. "Nice coverage from the hometown paper," he mumbled. "Car-rie, please tell Allison I'm going to miss my appointment in her classroom. I'm going down to the *Herald* to talk to Homer Spurlin."

"Are you sure? You two have missed so many times," she said, surprised.

"I know. Tell her I'll reschedule," Joe said, pulling on his coat and head-ing out the door.

SKYPE CONFERENCE

"I've got a fashion question for you," Kristi told Sutt. "Joe's not answering."

"Sure. Since I'm not a shoppy anymore, I'm *GQ*."

Kristi said a mother had complained about the clothes worn by a sixth-grade teacher. "Basically, the mom is complaining that her son's teacher wears too many thongs. As in underwear. What should I do with that?"

"You can probably imagine the responses running through my head, Kristi, but I'm going to leave them there. Have you seen her dress inappropriately?"

"No, but I'm not in there to see whatever she is doing when the class is seeing her underwear. I do know she's a really good teacher."

"If she's good, she won't have a problem with you telling her she needs to make some changes. I'm glad it's not me or some guy having to. That's awkward."

"It still makes me a little uncomfortable, telling her what to wear," Kristi said.

"I think you're too worried about it. A parent raised the issue, which is legitimate. If it is affecting the kids—and let's be honest, it would have affected me and a lot of others as sixth graders—then she needs to know. You're just passing along information that she needs to have."

"You're probably right. I just can't believe some of what comes my way."

"Speaking of that, I've got one for you," Sutt said. He explained Oswald's substitute-teacher shortage and that the district had begun approving professional leave requests only after substitutes were secured. "We're looking closely at student scores and avoidable teacher absences, and a lot are denied because we can't find good subs who can actually teach."

Sutt said his freshman teachers had avoided much of the problem by covering for each other and through interdisciplinary teaming. "One of the really good subs in the area has a blog where she rates schools. She's critical of just about everything—except our freshman wing."

Sutt said the blog included scathing comments about many schools, but particularly some in the Oswald district. She assailed the quality of lesson plans provided for substitute teachers, school lunches, student behavior, building cleanliness, and so on. "She doesn't use names, but everyone knows who she's talking about. No one has said we *can't* hire her, but I've had people in my face about why our freshman team keeps inviting her back."

"And what have you told them?"

"That she's a damn good substitute and we're short on good ones."

"So what's the issue?"

Sutt said many felt the district needed to show solidarity and that she should not be welcome in any Oswald building. "I said something about 'if the shoe fits' to an assistant principal from another building and he called me an asshole, right to my face!"

"I think you need to ask Rudy for some guidance."

"I did. He said as the leader of the freshman wing, it is up to me. So, am I a bad team player if I keep bringing her back? It's not my fault my team is good, she's a good sub, and she likes working in my freshman wing, right?"

Kristi wasn't sure. She argued that Sutt needed to show some unity with the rest of the Oswald staff, especially with Rudy working to establish a new, positive tone. "I'm surprised he would allow that division."

"I think he wants to keep my freshman teachers moving forward. We're his favorites. Unless he tells me I can't have her back, I say screw 'em. It's an instructional issue. I'm trying to make sure the kids still learn when the regular teacher is gone. Plus, I read her blog and she's right about a lot of it."

"I was just thinking of the politics of it. I didn't think of it in terms of instructional leadership," Kristi admitted. "Maybe you're right."

"Speaking of that, whatever happened with that old warhorse you were fighting with over homework?"

"You know, that one is interesting," Kristi said. "She was on the cycle for evaluation this year, which is a good thing. I would have wanted to evaluate her anyway, but if I had *put* her on the cycle, she would have felt like she was under attack."

Kristi said her initial walkthroughs and observations were rough. "The objectives were hard to follow and I could rarely see a point to what she was doing, unless it was to occupy time until music or recess or rigid control." Then she described a breakthrough moment.

"I was describing what I had seen in her room and trying to ask her some questions that would get her reflecting, but she kept coming back to 'these kids today.' Finally, I asked if she had lost her enthusiasm for teaching. She said yes and I told her I thought I could help with that."

Sutt was stunned. "Damn. You *are* hardcore! Even I have more tact."

Kristi said since that moment, she and the teacher had been communicating openly and honestly. Kristi had provided her with a couple of books and some online resources that she seemed to like. "She's not the best teacher I've got, but there's awareness now. I just said what I was thinking in a moment of unfiltered honesty and things have been better. Not perfect, but she's reflecting about her job, asking people to observe . . . even partnering with that first-year teacher who is struggling with management. I think she respected the honesty, even if it wasn't what she wanted to hear. Caught us both by surprise. It might be the best thing that has happened to me, except for my new boyfriends on the construction crew!" she laughed. "It was a big moment for me being a little more open."

They spent a little more time catching up on their lives outside of school. Kristi was preparing for a Thanksgiving Day marathon, something Sutt said he couldn't understand. Sutt and his wife were enjoying "not being broke at the end of the month," though he complained that his doubled salary didn't go as far as expected. They planned to try to check in with Joe in the next couple of days.

QUESTIONS

1. Evaluate Joe's handling of the fight involving Hayes, Smith, and Shottenkirk.
2. Assess Joe's latest interaction with Pat Patrazzo.
3. How should Joe respond to Gene DeVore's concern about the poetry unit? Does DeVore's status as a board member change anything?
4. Assess Joe's decision to address the pregame prayer with Coach Den Herder.
5. How should principals handle having their own children in the building?
6. How should Joe handle Jeralyn's Watch List?
7. Assess Joe's reaction to the article in the *Pinicon Herald*.
8. How should Kristi handle the elementary teacher's underwear?
9. Should Sutt continue to hire the substitute teacher who is critical of so many teachers?

Chapter Fifteen

Mid-November

The Media, the Mentee, the Abyss, and the Bandit

THOMAS JEFFERSON SAID . . .

After visiting Homer Spurlin at the *Pinicon Herald*, Joe stopped at Walsh Furniture and Design to see Claire and to vent. He dropped onto an over-stuffed recliner on the showroom floor and complained about the article, which she had already seen. "You can't be surprised, Joe. Newspaper people want to sell papers, even here. And it's the closest thing they have to a story."

"But it came across so negatively and made me seem out of touch."

"I don't think so," Claire countered. "You seemed like a principal who is trying to make things work and send a positive message. That's what principals do. What you said matched Zylstra and Mitchell. Aren't leaders supposed to supply the vision? What are you doing down here, anyway? Checking on work study students?"

Joe replayed his conversation with Homer Spurlin at the *Herald*.

Claire looked up from the wallpaper samples she was sorting. "You just came from the *newspaper*? About the article? Good God, Joe."

"I just told them I was disappointed by the tone and that it was unnecessarily negative. *Bush League* is what I wanted to say. Isn't the local paper supposed to support the school?"

"You probably came across as petty. Didn't Thomas Jefferson say to count to ten if you're mad and one hundred if you're really mad? You had no business going down there. Seriously, Joe. Now you're gonna tell Homer how to do his job?" she asked, shaking her head and noticing that a customer had come in.

Claire changed the subject in a direction that bothered Joe more. Speaking in a soft voice she said, "That was all wrong. Do you think you can fix things just with your will? We never have time to do anything together as a family, but you drop everything and give Homer Spurlin hell. The rest of us are a distant second. I wish you paid as close attention to us as to the stupid newspaper article."

She turned and walked across the showroom, greeting the customer in a friendly customer service voice. Joe was stung as he stood among the wallpaper samples. He wanted to push back and tell her she didn't understand, that she couldn't understand because she wasn't in his shoes, but pushing back was what took him to Spurlin's office. He had been served notice that despite months of trying to balance work and family, he wasn't getting it done. It was a bad day, maybe worse than the accident in the shop.

NO EXPLANATION

The news about the explosion that killed ten marines in the Middle East so close to Thanksgiving was everywhere. Every time the news told stories of injured and killed soldiers, thoughts in Pinicon invariably turned to community members who were serving in the military. For some reason, this one struck Helen McCallister differently. So differently that she left her class, drove to the banks of the Pinicon River, and watched the snow fall across her windshield for an entire gray afternoon.

Joe had been in special-education meetings most of the day and only found out about Helen's absence at home that night. The students had apparently taken attendance and maintained enough order in her classes all afternoon to avoid detection. A parent had called the Kessler Central Office and informed Mitchell.

"So this teacher is gone all afternoon and you don't even know?" Mitchell asked over the phone. "How does that happen in a building your size?"

Joe didn't have an answer, other than to say he had been swamped all afternoon.

"Tell McCallister this was her freebie. If she pulls that kind of thing again, she's done."

He told Mitchell that he had already left a message at Helen's home and that he would talk to her first thing in the morning.

Joe saw Helen as a solid but not stunning teacher. She had some creativity, as evidenced by her idea to invite Joe and some community members to join her Great Books class for the reading of *The Things They Carried*. Her courses were well organized and usually drew good work from students. Joe was shocked that she had made such an out-of-character move.

Before school the next morning, Helen offered no reason other than how hard the story hit her. "I lost my son nineteen years ago this month, close to the holidays like this, but it was cancer. That story just hit me today, like an out-of-body experience. I know that sounds weird." She said that before she knew what was happening, she was sitting in her car, watching snow fall across the river. "I know it was inexcusable and I have no real explanation. And I'm so sorry."

"I know it was completely out of character and I know how big your heart for kids is. Obviously, it is a good thing you have such good kids in your classes. If something bad had happened, we'd be in a lot of trouble," Joe said. "You need to know that Don Mitchell was very upset. Another absence like that would probably cost you your job."

Joe urged Helen to consider the district's employee-assistance program. "I'm not trying to get into your business. I know sometimes it helps to have a different set of ears. For what it's worth, if I can help at all, don't hesitate. I may not have the answers, but I'll sure listen." She seemed to appreciate his offer. He hoped she knew it was sincere.

He also hoped she knew that Mitchell was serious. How Mitchell could talk about terminating McCallister while allowing Merle Richards to masquerade as an industrial tech teacher was another matter that made no sense to Joe. McCallister was a hardworking, veteran teacher with a good record of going above and beyond. Richards was a constant headache. Joe vowed to take the discrepancy up with Mitchell at the next opportunity.

IF YOU BURN OUT, WE ALL LOSE

Joe needed to follow up with Allison Jesup about Gene DeVore's concerns with the poetry unit. He wanted to maintain her enthusiasm but also worried that she was working far too hard. Judging from time in her classroom, her lessons were top notch. It was the energy and effort she was spending that concerned Joe.

Allison looked frazzled, having taken on a couple of junior high coaching responsibilities, in addition to launching a Model UN program and National

Novel Writing Month. Joe usually saw her car in the lot shortly after 6:00 a.m. and as late as 9:00 p.m. He stopped by her room after school with a brownie from the foods class. His main objective was to gently suggest that she back off a bit because he worried about her burning out, but he also wanted to talk about the poems. "So, are you staying afloat?" Joe asked.

"I'm somewhere between two days and twenty minutes ahead of the students," Allison sighed. "That's probably not a good answer to give your principal."

"But it's honest. I've been there. Are you having fun?"

Allison said teaching was more fun than she expected. "One day, they're so far beyond what I expected and the next I get a blank stare. Drives me crazy, and I have to scrap a lot of my plans, but the kids do energize me. I'm glad I haven't figured my hourly wage!"

Joe laughed and said calculating hourly wages was a bad thing for an educator to do. He had once estimated his coaching salary to be less than 30 cents an hour. "You're doing great work. Be patient and know that you are laying a foundation. Everything you do won't be perfect this year. In fact, it never will be and doesn't have to be. You're establishing yourself."

Allison said she had been thinking a lot about how to keep her perfectionist tendencies in check. Joe cautioned that those tendencies could be a blessing and a curse. "On one hand, I want you to have very high expectations of yourself and students. But perfectionism can drag you down when things fall short of your possibly unrealistic expectations. We can beat ourselves up."

Changing the subject, Joe asked how students had reacted to the poetry unit. "Oh! It was awesome! Intense. We were deep into government, taxes, war, love, racism, you name it. Those were some of the unexpectedly good days! I wish you could have seen it!"

"Actually, I do too. Sounds exciting. Kudos to you for pushing them to think and share. Interestingly enough, I talked to one parent who was concerned about some of what the kids produced and were reading. Some similar feelings came up in the article in the *Pinicon Herald*."

She seemed surprised by the objections and had not seen the *Herald* article. "Actually, most of the stuff in the paper is so poorly written that I don't bother. Plus, I'm too busy," she said, pointing to piles around the room. "I used to be organized."

"I want you to do two things," Joe said. "First, I'd like to see you cut your hours back. I love the work ethic, but it has to be sustainable. I don't want you to burn out. Keep your goals but with less emphasis on perfection. This won't be your best year of teaching, just maybe your hardest." Allison nodded.

"The second thing is to realize that not everyone is ready for your approach. You saw that with the poems and the issues they brought out. There are a lot of things people aren't ready for."

"If you're asking me to back off the edgy stuff, you'll want to look at some of these books I want to use," she said, handing him a second-semester reading list.

"I'm not telling you to back off at all. I just want you to have a clear rationale prepared and to think about the setup—alignment with the curriculum, ground rules, and goals. And be ready for questions—that's all. And maybe run it past a mentor, like Mark Watters or me."

Joe could see her wheels turning and wondered if she would heed his advice about her hours. "Now, it's after four. I want you to get out of here," he said, gesturing toward the door.

CUT

Joe was sure that using a tiny video camera during classroom observations was one of the best things he'd done as principal. Though some teachers were uncomfortable with it, others enjoyed it. Among those who were comfortable was Charity Hampton, whose band rehearsals Joe always found energizing. Despite inexperience with some curricular areas, he told teachers he could certainly recognize well-prepared, enthusiastic teachers who were intent on moving kids forward. And the video recorder helped him capture and share those moments.

Hampton had told Joe that her overarching objective as a music teacher was to generate interest and enthusiasm, whether that yielded skillful musicians or merely adults who enjoyed music. Her secondary goal was to "produce and perform high-quality music." Though she was often rigid and standoffish, her skill as a teacher was unmistakable. Joe felt certain he could entice her into participating in some interdisciplinary teaching next year. He had floated the idea of studying art, music, literature, and history of the 1960s, and she seemed curious.

As he observed the rehearsal, Joe wished more students experienced the kind of instruction she was leading. The band was working on tunes from *West Side Story*. After they played as a large group, she stopped and asked individual sections to play while she walked to different places in the room.

Her style reminded him of intense, energetic coaches he had known. "Trumpets, I want you to *listen* to the winds here. It needs to sound light, floaty. See if it floats. Winds, let's go from 24. . . ."

After working individual sections, she recorded the full band. "Better, better. I like it. Now hang with me. Instruments down. I want you to relax and listen to this next piece. Contrast it with what you just played. You haven't seen the film, so tell me what kind of *scene* the music creates in your mind. What's the picture? Quiet and listen, eyes closed. . . ."

As Joe sat, eyes closed, an urgent text from Carrie interrupted his concentration. *NEED U OFFICE NOW!!* His heart jumped, knowing how closely Carrie protected his time in classrooms. He hated to leave, but strode out of the room just as the jazz band took up "Maria."

His mind raced through a few of the reasons Carrie might have summoned him. None were positive. As he briskly rounded the corner, he saw Robin Stiles seated in front of his desk, her once long, jet-black dyed hair now cropped short. "She just walked in and sat down in your office. Didn't say a word," Carrie whispered.

Joe pulled up a chair and grabbed a Diet Coke from the mini-fridge. "It's good to have you back, Robin. Can I get you something?"

"No, thanks," she said softly.

"How is your second day back with us?" Joe asked, wondering what he should say.

After a long pause, Robin said, "Well, I'm here. That's worth something, right?"

"It is. And we're glad you are," Joe said, trying to sound sincere without pity. "Can I help with anything? Or do you just need some time? You're welcome here anytime. Mrs. Kramer was sure sorry to be out for surgery right when you came back."

Robin looked up. "I just . . . I don't think I can do this. I don't think I can be here. The meds they're making me take . . . I just don't know. . . ."

Joe let her talk, and resisted peppering her with questions. Jeralyn always said that adults had to learn to be comfortable with silence when engaging kids. He figured she would talk if she wanted to. If not, she could just hang out. She offered a few details about her hospital stay, which sounded miserable, but she seemed comfortable talking with him and letting her emotions out.

"Does jumping right back into school feel like too much?" Joe asked.

"That's it. I don't want to be in that fuckin' hospital; I don't want to be at home, don't really want to be here. And I don't want to feel like this."

Before he could respond, Robin grabbed a newly sharpened pencil from his desk and jammed it into her left forearm, opening a gash. As the pencil splintered, she turned her forearm toward the desk and slammed it against what was left of the pencil, blood spurting.

"Robin, whoa!" Joe shouted, wishing he had not been so loud. Robin grimaced, cursed, and flailed with both arms as Joe came beside her. He reached and tried to steady her arms, now speaking in a much lower tone of voice. "Hey . . . breathe, easy. Give me your arm." She was sweaty, ashen, and cold.

Carrie was already in the room with the first aid kit, although blood from Robin's arm was no match for the gauze she had grabbed from the kit. "We need a towel or something and get the nurse," Joe said, still clutching Robin's elbows. Examining the pencil wound, Joe saw other fresh cuts that had reopened on her arms. Robin was now sobbing, limp, and bleeding.

Carrie produced a towel and began dabbing at Robin's cuts since the girl seemed to have no more energy for hurting herself or resisting. "I'm sorry," she whimpered as Carrie eased her back into the chair while Joe pressed the towels into her arms.

"Don't you worry, baby, just sit here with me," Carrie soothed.

Ten minutes had gone by and Joe had started to go to look for the nurse, Rose Johnson, when she rounded the corner into the office, clicking off her cell phone. "What's up?" she asked, her voice trailing off as she caught sight of the blood on all three of them and Carrie tending to the slumping Robin. Joe felt his eyes burn through Rose as she quickened her pace to attend to the girl.

THE RICE KRISPIES BANDIT

Early the next morning, Joe found a handwritten note from food-service manager Marcella Ramirez in his mailbox, asking him to come to the kitchen as soon as he arrived. He could hear the cooks bantering as he made his way through the maze of stoves and equipment. "Marcella, I assume you have a hot pan of cinnamon rolls coming out of the oven that you need me to test," he announced as he came around the corner.

"Just one. The rest are for the bus drivers."

"I sure appreciate how well you take care of those guys. And me. Actually, everybody."

Marcella smiled. Joe had been surprised to learn that Jerry Hughes had scarcely set foot in the kitchen during his years at Pinicon. From the day in September when Joe donned an apron and helped serve food, he felt his rapport build steadily with Marcella and the cooks.

While Joe started on his cinnamon roll, Marcella said she discovered five boxes of Rice Krispies were missing. She had stayed late after school the day before to meet with the oven repairman and said she had seen some kids hanging around the cafeteria when she left. "Are they supposed to be in here after school?"

"I've told Brenton Michaels and some kids who are trying to start a video game club they can meet here."

"Well, they weren't doing anything but wasting time and cussing when I was here. Some of these kids don't care who's around. They just act like they own the place," Marcella complained. "Anyway, I left the repairman to finish up. I'll bet anything they were in here and stole the Rice Krispies and who knows what else. I haven't checked everything yet."

Joe nodded, trying to seem interested, though the missing Rice Krispies were already low on his list of priorities. Still, Marcella felt it was important enough to report and Joe needed to respect that and respond accordingly. "I will certainly do some asking around. Let me know if there is anything else missing. And thank God nobody took the stuff for the cinnamon rolls. That would change a lot of things," Joe said, winking at the laughing cooks.

Joe checked with several coaches, teachers, and students who had stayed after school the day before. No one reported seeing any students in the cafeteria other than Brenton Michaels and the video gamers for any length of time. He reached head custodian Dave Crawford on the radio. "I'm up here on the roof on the south wing," Crawford said. He was visibly surprised when Joe squeaked open the hatch that led onto the roof and stepped out. "I'm not big on heights, so I won't stay long up here," Joe said. Crawford said he was trying the third or fourth repair on another elusive roof leak.

"If you hang around too long, I'm gonna put you to work," Crawford said, smiling from beneath his Ford Mustang cap.

Crawford said he had only seen Brenton's group, a few cheerleaders, Marcella, and the repairman. "I helped the repair guy slide the oven back in place when he was done. That thing's a brute. Probably ought to replace it, since he's down here every few weeks."

Joe told him to contact the Kessler Central Office if he and Marcella felt the oven needed to be replaced. "No sense wasting time on it if it's shot."

Crawford confirmed that the cafeteria area was empty when he and the repairman left together. Joe thanked him for his detective and maintenance work, opened the hatch, and climbed down the ladder into the building, chilled from a biting November wind. The Rice Krispies caper looked like a dead end and Joe doubted that he would spend much more time on it, beyond a few quick questions to Brenton Michaels's gamers.

He thought about Professor Summers's admonition that the cooks, custodians, secretaries, and bus drivers really make the school run. "People will notice if they are gone long before they realize the principal is," he said. This was also the first group the professor suggested building relationships with.

Joe thought he had built fairly solid relationships with the cooks, custodians, bus drivers, and secretaries. Perhaps it was his teasing relationship with Carrie, the donuts for the bus drivers, helping the cooks serve food, or joking with Dave Crawford about problems with his beloved Ford Mustang. Whatever the reason, Joe felt as comfortable dealing with them as with anyone at Pinicon. Why, then, was he hesitant to tell Crawford that the dip of chewing tobacco he always had in his lower lip was a violation of the state's tobacco-free schools law?

FULL ESCORT

Joe hated to bother Jeralyn so soon after her surgery. Her husband answered her mobile phone. "No bother, she'll want to talk to you," he said. She was awake and interested in what had happened with Robin Stiles. Joe explained that he had spoken to Robin's parents, who picked her up and promised to take her to the Pinicon Medical Clinic.

"Her parents have to work and can't take any time off. She can't stay home, and insurance won't cover any more time in the hospital. I don't know if that's true, but it's what they said."

"It's probably right," Jeralyn speculated.

"So we agreed that dad will drop her off at school at 7:15. Carrie or I will meet her at the front door and take her to the office until school starts. When classes start, she's going to have someone with her all the time—walking her to class, to the bathroom, whatever. At least until we figure out if she needs more treatment or something. I've got no idea what else to do. We've gotta get special ed involved to get her some help."

"Joe, she's not a special-ed student. Her mental-health issues are separate. And you and Carrie can't do all that escorting," Jeralyn protested.

"What do you mean separate? The girl needs help and she can't go back to the hospital!"

"In this state, those are separate issues, unless she's evaluated and approved for special-ed services, and good luck getting mom and dad to sign off on that. I worked for months to convince them to get her to the hospital," Jeralyn said. "It breaks my heart that I can't be there. You guys are going to have to do the best you can with her until I get back."

Joe said he and Carrie planned to do what they could and assign the rest of the escort duties to teacher aides.

"What about Rose? She could do some of it."

Joe said that when Carrie called, Rose was eating lunch. "Helen McCallister was in Rose's office when Carrie called and said we needed her ASAP. Rose said she wasn't interrupting her break for another kid wanting a Tylenol. Rose told me Carrie didn't make it clear that it was an *emergency*. I heard Carrie on the phone calling her, so I know that's BS. But I got her attention and she knows what ASAP means now."

Jeralyn warned that teachers would be uncomfortable having Robin in class and that they might see constant escorts as inappropriate and impractical. Joe agreed, but said until something else could be arranged, that was the plan. He told Jeralyn to double up her meds and hurry back. "Yesterday was only the second day with you gone. We've got some holes in the dam," he said.

SKYPE CONFERENCE

"I didn't know pay phones still existed. When was the last time you saw one?" Sutt asked, describing the bomb threat that came in to Oswald High School a couple of days earlier. He said a freshman Oswald student who had been in an ongoing dispute with student teachers in the Freshman Writing Center had called in the threat. "He's kind of a mousy kid. Doesn't look like a bomber."

"So you're a profiler now? What does a bomber look like?" Joe asked sarcastically.

"I mean he doesn't look like a kid you'd expect to see busted on felony terrorism charges."

After the student had gotten belligerent with the writing center staff, Sutt had suspended him from school for two days and from the writing center indefinitely. The same afternoon, he called in a bomb threat to the Oswald High School office. "Thankfully we had dismissed for the day. The number went to a pay phone out at the state park. Our school resource officer drove out there and talked to some hikers who saw him. The cops were waiting for him when he showed up for his job at the mall. Ballgame. That will teach him not to screw with my writing center!"

Sutt also described efforts to improve communication with the Oswald police after a gang-related shooting a week earlier. "An alternative high school kid who used to go here got shot and killed. All the kids know him and the shooter. We've got counselors all over the place, but kids are afraid to talk. Rudy has been meeting nonstop with our SRO and the police chief trying to get them to share information more quickly. Now I have a list of kids the cops think are gang affiliated. It's about twice as long as I thought. What's up with you guys?"

Kristi began. "I think I alienated a couple of board members and a few of my teachers."

"Alienating people like the maintenance staff is Sutt's job," Joe snickered.

Kristi said a group of teachers and board members had attended a conference on developing student leadership. The conference, which was paid for by the Winthrop Partners in Education, featured different initiatives, ranging from university-developed programs to teacher- and community-led efforts and commercially produced products.

"The super wanted me to go, but it has been a long time since the teachers here had any opportunities like that, so I really pushed for teachers to go and convinced him. They came back pretty excited about Leadership Stars. Have you heard of it?"

"Was that the company that got in trouble for inflated claims of how well kids were doing with their reading program or something like that?" Joe asked.

"That's it," Kristi said. "When they presented it to me, I listened politely and told them about that. I said I was more interested in them developing our own program."

"So they came back excited and felt like you didn't listen," Sutt summarized.

"Exactly. They asked why I sent them in the first place if I already knew what I wanted. I was trying to build them up and say we have the expertise to develop our own program, but that's not how they took it."

"Too bad. Can you convince them that's what you meant?" Joe asked.

"I think so, but for now our shared decision-making took a few steps back. Some of them think I'm being military top-down all of the sudden. It's discouraging."

"Maybe you have to take the blame, apologize for the misunderstanding, and go out of your way to convince them you're not a dictator," Sutt said. "Rudy says sometimes the leader has to take more of the blame than is fair for the sake of the followers."

"I agree. My coach always talked about the difference between being disappointed and being discouraged. He said being discouraged was more serious because it signals a broken spirit. But disappointment is *temporary*, like I wish things had gone differently, but there's another game to play, another chance. I think he's right. You're disappointed, but ready to move forward."

Joe shared the Rice Krispies bandit story with the group, though he wasn't sure why. It certainly was not the biggest thing on his radar. Sutt threw his head back. "I swear, Joe, you are in Utopia chasing five boxes of missing cereal while Kristi has a near mutiny and I have a bomb threat."

"Not so fast, Sutt. It isn't all rainbows and butterflies here," Joe said, describing the Confederate flag fight and negative article in the *Pinicon Herald*.

"That flag thing seems like it could really blow up. Is it over?" Kristi asked.

"For now at least. I haven't seen any more. Just a couple on cars in the parking lot," Joe said.

"The courts say you could get at those too," Sutt said. "They caused a disruption. You and the counselor are feeling the tension. Big fight in the cooking class. You could tell 'em to take the stickers off or park somewhere else."

They debated the wisdom of Sutt's suggestion for a few minutes before Joe changed the subject. "Here's something minor but has been on my mind. My head custodian is awesome, but he always has a dip of chewing tobacco in his lip. I've been meaning to say something to him, but it never seems like the right time. I don't want to damage the relationship."

"I don't see why you have to," Kristi said. "Don't make it about the two of you. Make it about the policy. Just tell him it's gonna get both of you in trouble if he keeps it up. You wouldn't let him smoke all the time, so how is this different?"

"I've thought about that," Joe admitted.

"Honestly, who cares?" Sutt asked. "He's a great guy who's in your corner. If no one has complained, I say let a sleeping dog lie. Is it lay or lie, Kristi?"

"I believe it's lie, Sutt."

"Right. Anyway, aren't there some superstars in every organization who are entitled to be left alone? I can't see how it's hurting anyone, so why risk alienating him? It's like the football prayer. Let it go. I think you leave those guys alone since they're doing such good work."

"Tom McHale, the elementary principal and my mentor, says I have to address it because everyone else notices. I think he's right. I'm not sure why I feel so bad redirecting people I like and who are doing good work, but I guess that's part of the deal."

Sutt changed the subject. "Kristi, don't take this wrong and maybe it's the computer, but you look really tired. My wife says never tell a woman she looks tired because women think it's like telling her she looks like hell. But you do look tired. You okay?"

Kristi laughed. "I *am* tired. And I *do* look like hell. The marathon training has been tough, but I'm fine. Just run down. I stay later and later but don't seem to get ahead. I'm counting the days until break. By the way, Sutt, you look absolutely dashing," she said.

QUESTIONS

1. Claire told Joe his trip to see Homer Spurlin at the *Pinicon Herald* was poor judgment. Do you agree?
2. How should Joe handle Helen McCallister's sudden and unusual absence from school?
3. Evaluate Joe's handling of Allison Jesup's poetry unit and his concerns about her risk for burnout.
4. How much time should Joe allocate to the missing Rice Krispies?
5. How should Joe proceed with Robin Stiles?
6. Did Kristi mishandle the teachers who returned from the conference?

7. Would Joe be overreaching if he took Sutt's advice and told students to remove the Confederate stickers from their vehicles or park elsewhere?

Chapter Sixteen

December

A Better Way?

80/20

In grad school, Joe had liked the idea that effective principals should spend the majority of their time with their best teachers. He agreed that interacting with the high flyers as much as possible was good for the teachers and principal alike. He had also heard a lot of practicing administrators warn how hard it was to do. Joe said Merle Richards proved they were right.

Sutt had given him software for tracking the way he had spent his time. Joe wondered if it might have been an illegal copy, but he used it anyway because he found it so useful. Days that were mostly consumed with management displayed in red while those heavy in leadership, or specifically *instructional* leadership, appeared in green.

It also displayed the names of individual teachers or students with whom Joe had been engaged at particular times. Looking over the results made him wonder what it would be like to have help from a school administration manager, lead teacher, or some other kind of assistant. Any help with routine duties that chewed up so much of his time would be good.

Zylstra was a few minutes early for a meeting in Joe's office. They had developed a solid working relationship and Joe was comfortable sharing honestly with her. He was excited to get her reaction to his time chart and hoped she wouldn't ask where he got the software.

"Related to our conversations about leading versus managing, here's how I've been tracking my time," Joe said, drawing her attention to his laptop.

"How does it compare to the way you *thought* you were spending it?"

"I know I do a lot of firefighting, but I didn't think it was quite this bad," he said, referring to the screen that was covered in red.

"It's great that you're working so hard to be in classrooms every day. I see evidence of a lot of walkthroughs, but those can become like fast food. Quick and easy, but not very good for you—or teachers and kids, especially if they're substitutes for deeper engagement and conversation."

Joe nodded and pointed to teachers' names that appeared throughout the red management category. "These guys are killing me," he said, pointing to Merle Richards, Stu Petersen, and Joyce Barry. "It's always something with them."

Zylstra said she found the Pareto Principle to be an accurate gauge of new principals' time. "Everything is out of whack. You have a small number of leeches that bleed away your time while things you really want to do go unattended. Plus, you're working hard to show you can handle the job. That often means *you think* you're practicing good *servant leadership* by taking care of all kinds of things for other people, but you might be enabling them and wasting time on things that don't help teachers teach and kids learn. And that can kill leadership."

Zylstra then shifted the conversation. "Of course, we can scold you for not spending enough time on leadership and instruction, but the teachers have to be *ready* for it. If they're used to shutting their doors and doing their own thing, you'll have a hard time. Are they ready?"

Joe said he felt most of the teachers were basically receptive to instructional leadership—and leadership in general. "Whether they think *I* can provide it might be another question."

"They've been doing things a certain way for a long time. And it's not like they were unsuccessful. Scores are good. Pinicon kids are doing pretty well. They may not have a lot of urgency. You'll spend a couple of years setting the stage for the things you want to do. I know Tom McHale has told you it's gonna take time," she said.

Joe smiled at the way mentoring conversations with Zylstra, McHale, and Professor Summers all had the same grounding effect. It was as if the three could exchange scripts and deliver the same message, regardless of the circumstances. Joe always left the conversations with a new focus and determination to do what Zylstra referred to as "the right work."

SATURDAY SCHOOL

Joe and the leadership team had met several times about the way detentions had been handled. Joe had been bothered by the number of detention students who sat idly with their heads down in classrooms or the office. He explained he wanted consequences for breaking rules that didn't rise to the suspension level, but that kids just mindlessly sitting around made no sense.

The leadership team tossed around several ideas and finally settled on Joe's suggestion that teachers should emphasize that detention time was to be spent doing something that was of benefit—cleaning, studying, *something.* As part of the process, the team examined discipline referrals from the previous three years and sorted offenses by category and teachers. Joe suggested giving all the data to the entire faculty, but several on the committee resisted, particularly Mark Watters. "I've got a real issue with that and others will, too. Teachers should only get their own data. If they want to share it, that's their business," he said.

The team ultimately recommended that Saturday School be assigned to students with more than two detentions in a given quarter. Once-a-month Saturday School sessions would be held at school and staffed by associates or teachers who would be paid a stipend. Teachers, along with Young, Joe, and head custodian Dave Crawford, would produce a monthly list of things that students could do during their Saturday School time. Students assigned to Saturday School who failed to attend would face in-school suspension.

Joe had hoped for an honest faculty conversation about office referrals, but McHale advised him to settle for what he could get. He wanted a few faculty members' referrals to be laid bare for all to see, but felt Saturday School was a good step forward and perhaps the leadership team was right— this should be kept private. Joe planned to use teachers' individual data for one-on-one conversations.

Joe was thrilled when Larry Den Herder offered to supervise the first Saturday School on the day of the Pirate Invitational Wrestling Tournament. Den Herder also wanted to donate his stipend to the Pirate Booster Club. Joe was frustrated when the Kessler Central Office said the money couldn't be transferred directly to the club. Instead, the coach would have to be paid, deposit his check, and then write a check to the booster club. All in all, Joe was glad to have a solid staff member like Den Herder take care of the first Saturday School, as it was one less thing for him to worry about. And Young was delighted to have some extra help with the tournament.

I CAN'T BELIEVE YOU CARE SO LITTLE

Despite her intensity and skill as a teacher, Joe thought Charity Hampton would be perfect for a role as an uptight teacher in a movie. Even her name seemed straight out of central casting. When Joe told the staff that he wanted each of them to feel that their curricular area was the single most important part of their students' days, he knew Charity would have no trouble with that outlook.

He also knew she would struggle with the second part of his challenge, which was to understand that everyone else saw their area in the same way. If teachers could adopt this "dual perspective," Joe said Pinicon had a chance to be a lively building that shared kids and offered many opportunities. He admired her skill as a musician and hoped he could help improve her people skills. He had hinted that he felt she alienated a lot of kids and teachers—a dangerous proposition for anyone trying to build a program that was invariably competing for students' time and attention.

Back in September, she had been angry when Joe decided students would not leave core classes for music lessons. "I'm not saying music is unimportant," he told the faculty, "but it's not good for students to be missing instructional time in core classes when we can do music lessons at other times." Charity protested vehemently in the faculty meeting, complaining that it was evidence of Joe's bias against the arts, but no one supported her.

Despite her insistence that scheduling individual lessons during noncore courses would never work, Joe, Carrie, and Charity had been able to do it. In fact, most lessons were five minutes longer. Despite this, Charity always had a list of requests and complaints for Joe.

The latest email from Charity was standard. She and the band had been practicing in the auditorium for a couple of weeks in preparation for the winter concert. She had wanted several items moved out of the backstage area, and Richards sent two boys from study hall to do so.

Joe,
HOW LONG do we have to wait for the crap on the stage to be moved back to Mr. Richards' shop? In the middle of rehearsal today, Austin Voss and Daniel Henshaw were sitting in the auditorium hall playing cards, laughing loudly. I sent them back to Mr. Richards' study hall because they were disruptive and disrespectful. How long until SOMEONE gets his study hall under control? Some of us are working.
Charity

Joe thanked her for letting him know and said she should feel comfortable telling Richards herself. She emailed back, saying that was not her role. Joe reminded her that open and honest communication between faculty members was essential to a healthy school and that it might be a while before he could take it up with Richards. When Joe asked Richards, he said he forgot that he had sent them to move the items and that they never returned to study hall.

Joe thought Austin Voss and Daniel Henshaw could have been the poster children for kids who feel stifled in school. Rough around the edges and uninterested in school, the boys were headaches but not bad kids. When Joe warned them about being respectful of the band's rehearsal, failing to return to study hall, and a likely suspension, Austin spoke up. "Since we're talking about respect, Ms. Hampton should give *us* some. Calling us idiots and asking if we have a brain isn't very respectful."

That's the way it so often went with Charity—escalating something minor into something major. "They were disruptive and not supposed to be there. I asked them if they had *brains* or were just idiots. Mr. Richards could stand to use his and manage his study hall, too," she said.

"Charity, those two will never be citizens of the year. They shouldn't have been there and I've talked to Merle about it. But if we want respect, we need to model it. Screaming at them to use their brains isn't going to help. The same is true for your comment about Mr. Richards."

"So this is my fault? Kids are AWOL, disrupting rehearsal, and *I'm* in the wrong?!"

The conversation continued for a few minutes as Charity cited a litany of examples of Joe's ineffectiveness, insisting that many kids were running wild through Pinicon. Joe tried to stay low key and repeated his suggestion that she could interact with more tact and finesse.

"We've got some outlaws getting off scot free from a gutless principal," Charity complained. "I told you three days ago that Juneau Hall threw open the cafeteria door so hard that it almost took my head off. And now I find out that you haven't even *talked* to him? I can't believe you care so little for my safety."

Although he was on fire inside, Joe was determined to stay above the fray. While she was certainly one of the most skilled teachers at Pinicon, he found her insufferable. He could do nothing right in her eyes and consequently avoided her.

"I said last fall that when you send a kid to me, I'll deal with it in the way I see fit. I understand that you're frustrated with my timing and action," he said.

"You mean *inaction*. I thought you cared at first," she interrupted.

Joe paused, choosing his words carefully. "Charity, you're a tremendous teacher, and I imagine you are stressed about the concert coming up. Understand that there are things you're unaware of that keep me from dealing with things on your timeline. Lots of them. As for caring, you have *no idea* what keeps me awake at night. No idea. So let's leave it there."

Fire pumping through his veins, he was glad he had kept his cool. He badly wanted to point out the irony in Charity calling for respect but walking away before he had finished speaking, but let it go.

THE BIRD IS THE WORD

Early in the year, Martha Mills and Greg Altman had proposed to the leadership team that students in good academic standing in study halls could apply to be teacher aides. This was music to everyone's ears. Many teachers could use the help, and none more than Martha, whose glacial speed at completing routine tasks irritated Joe.

The downside was that students uninterested in being teacher aides and not taking courses available from Kessler tended to languish in study halls. It was no wonder Joe had frequent problems with kids like Juneau Hall, Brenton Michaels, Austin Voss, and Daniel Henshaw, who had nothing to do in study hall. Weak study hall supervisors like Merle Richards compounded the problem. This was another issue on which he needed help from the leadership team.

Dalton Myerly was one such idle ninth grader who had come to Mills's classroom from study hall to work on a research paper. Instead, he created a graphic of the Kessler High School logo with a hand with the middle finger extended over it and added the text, "Ride this, Kessler!" With a few disturbingly easy key strokes, Dalton installed it as the wallpaper across the Pinicon network.

Despite the prank being the talk of the day, it escaped Joe until after school when he overheard Juneau Hall complaining about what would happen if he had done something similar. When Joe walked into the computer lab and saw all twenty-seven computers illuminated with the gesture and graphics, he was shocked that it had remained there so long. Martha Mills was huddled over her own computer with manuals and computer books strewn across her desk.

"Martha, I just heard about this. What's going on?"

"Mr. Myerly's handiwork. I don't know how he did it or how to get rid of it."

How did she not see what Dalton was doing? How did she fail to see it on the screens for most of the day? And shouldn't a computer teacher be able to fix it quickly? He was intent on removing Dalton's wallpaper, even if it meant shutting down the whole network.

Joe called Ernie Johansen, the driver of Dalton's bus. "Tell me where you are, Ernie, and pull over. I'm coming to get Dalton Myerly." Ernie gave his location and Joe roared out of town in Young's Camaro after the bus.

Joe did all the talking on the way back to school. He told Dalton he could be charged with a host of crimes for misuse of school equipment and added something about the time Martha Mills had spent trying to remove the wallpaper, divided by her salary and a few other things that came into his head. Blowing smoke, he told Dalton all of this could be a serious crime. He hoped to scare Dalton into remorse and taking the wallpaper down if Martha had not figured out how. He told Dalton he could probably keep the discipline within the school and not let it turn into "a law enforcement issue" if he got the wallpaper down immediately.

Martha had made little progress when Joe returned to the lab with the ashen-faced Dalton. With Martha looking over his shoulder, he returned the Pinicon Pirate logo to the computers in a few minutes while Martha jotted down notes. Back in his office, Joe had Dalton call home and tell his mom why he had not come home on the bus and that she would need to come and get him. While they waited for her, Joe piled a little more on Dalton.

"You know, a lot of Kessler kids have probably heard about this and don't think it's funny. I hope they don't take it out on you, outside of school. I can control a lot of what happens at school, but outside of school is different."

He told Dalton that he would be banned from using the school's computers until at least the fourth quarter and that he would personally apologize to Martha Mills and Ernie Johansen for the disruption. "You don't have to thank me for not making this a legal issue, but you're lucky I didn't. Past that, you'll be serving an all-day Saturday School."

Dalton's eyes were wide.

TECH-ACHE

Kessler High School principal Cal Murphy called to let Joe know that some students had started a Facebook page called "CreepWatch" that identified sex offenders who were family members of Kessler and Pinicon students. "They started tweeting about a dad who is on the registry. It got messy and we had a few fights over it today."

"This tech stuff is killing me," Joe complained before telling Murphy about Dalton Myerly's wallpaper stunt. He was shocked that Murphy already knew because it had also appeared on several computers at KHS, but Kessler's technology director had removed it quickly. Then Joe explained what he had done with Myerly.

"That's a helluva good bluff. You hit him with a little of everything . . . a felony, some Kessler vigilantes, and you got to play good cop! Isn't it scary what these kids can do?"

"It's crazy, but we don't have a tech director," Joe said. "We really need support there."

"Speaking of tech, Mitchell has been on me about banning cell phones from the building," Murphy said. "He doesn't understand that it would be just about unenforceable. But he's not the one who would have to do it. Don't be surprised if that's his next great idea for Pinicon."

Joe thanked Murphy for the heads-up and asked him to send a copy of his message to teachers about CreepWatch. Next, he dialed Tom McHale to see if it had reached the elementary building and if he knew anything about Mitchell's idea to ban cell phones.

QUESTIONER IN CHIEF

Joe wanted to make sure the December faculty meeting produced as much lively discussion as usual, but also wanted to keep it light with home holiday cheer. As a result he had laid out a red tablecloth and Christmas cookies Claire had sent with him. He was happy to see that the signup sheet Helen McCallister had circulated had yielded a table full of holiday treats. He had purchased coffee cups with the Pinicon logo on them for each faculty and staff member, which were customized to say things like "Teaching the Pinicon Way," depending on each person's job, and placed them at their tables.

"After you've stocked up on a few thousand extra calories, I invite you to settle in for today's conversation." Joe had assigned the faculty into their regular groups, with a member of the leadership team at each table. Throughout the fall, he had begun every monthly faculty meeting with one of his discussion starters, such as the purpose of school, the definition of an educated person, and the ongoing effort to define the Pinicon Way.

After a few awkward sessions in the beginning, teachers began telling him they looked forward to the sessions, even though sometimes tense and pointed exchanges about philosophical issues had become routine. Joe always prefaced the discussions by reminding them of Roland Barth's assertion that the quality of a school is closely related to the kinds of relationships among the adults who work there.

Emphatically turning off his cell phone, Joe began, "We all know that teaching is a mix of science and art. Today our topic is how we know what lesson our students need next." Joe had wanted to pose the question ever since Pat Patrazzo had stuffed lesson plans for the entire year into his mailbox in August. Joe circulated among the tables, listening.

Mark Watters touted the use of "common formative assessments to guide next steps" and Larry Den Herder agreed. "It is just like watching game film. I've got to watch Friday night's game film to know what we need in practice on Monday." June Ramsey said she didn't have much time for formative assessment, since her role was to provide support to regular ed teachers. Allison Jesup described a questionnaire used at the beginning of each unit to assess students' knowledge of the topic. "A lot of things they know are just wrong. It's like they thought *Forrest Gump* was a documentary," she said to hearty laughter. Stu Petersen said the next lesson depended on "whether we can go outside and gym scheduling conflicts" to more laughter, while Pat Patrazzo said his next lessons were the "result of experience and a time-tested curriculum guide."

As the ten-minute mark approached, teachers were engaged in lively discussion, so he let them go on. A few were packing up their things at 4 p.m., the end of contract time. "I want to thank you for your time and engagement. Remember, it may not seem like we ever have closure to these meetings, but we're setting a stage for the future and what we mean by the Pinicon Way. This is a *process* and I'm so encouraged by the way you've approached it."

As the group started to break up, Rhonda Prior stood up. "Mr. Gentry, we often wonder what you think when we're sitting here going at each other. We're glad you emphasize that this takes time. And we want to thank you for making it a priority. Several of us have been at this a while, but have never had the opportunity to talk about these things. We know over the long haul, it's going to make us better. And for that, we thank you," she said, handing him a $100 gift card to the bakery in Kessler. "The cooks said you like cinnamon rolls," she said with a laugh.

He was touched by the gesture and told them so. The sessions always energized him, but this one felt like a much-needed affirmation of his efforts. Prior's statement on behalf of the faculty indicated that they too saw the efforts as time well spent. Most encouraging was that several remained twenty minutes after the meeting was officially adjourned. He could have stood around for another hour, talking about teaching and holiday plans and eating Christmas cookies.

LET ME WARN YOU ABOUT THE OLD LADY

Dave Myerly was sitting in the outer office when Joe returned from the meeting. Unlike his unimposing son, Dave was a stout 6' 4", dressed in dungarees, work boots, and a Chicago Bears sweatshirt. Joe wasn't sure whether the December weather or Dave's emotions were the reason for his unusually red cheeks. He hoped it was the former.

"Everybody cleared out of this place. I thought I was the only one left," Dave said, extending his hand and introducing himself.

"Carrie goes home at four and the teachers and I were in a meeting that ran long. Sorry you were waiting. I'm the principal, Joe Gentry. My friends call me Joe. Happy to meet you."

Dave said he had come to talk about "this computer thing with Dalton" and that he had "been round and round on it" with his ex-wife, Dalton's mother. "We share custody, but that's about it. She and I don't agree on much when it comes to him. He's with her this weekend and I know she won't bring him for that Saturday School. I'd like to see discipline like it used to be. Knock 'em upside the head! But I know you can't do that no more."

Joe thanked him for his support and noted how easy it had been for Dalton to create and deactivate the wallpaper. "A lot of the kids have better computer skills than the adults," Joe said.

"And a lot of the adults let the damn computer raise the kid," Dave offered. "That's exactly what is happening with my ex and her boyfriend. Some computer guy she met online."

A complicated family dynamic was taking shape. Maybe more than Joe wanted to know.

Joe thanked him again for coming in and for his support and explained that Dalton would be suspended at school if he didn't attend Saturday School. Joe also said he would call Dalton's mother to make sure everyone was on the same page.

After walking Dave to the parking lot door, the squeak of basketball shoes lured Joe into the gym—a good respite for him. As he watched Elliott's team practice, he wondered about the difficulty of being the principal's child. A couple of months earlier, Elliott had complained that some people seemed to be waiting for him to screw up and others seemed to think he should be twice as good as other kids. Joe and Claire worried whether some thought Elliott enjoyed special treatment. Nearly halfway through the school year, their son appeared to have only a few friends and seemed to be socially on the outside looking in. But was that because of Joe's job or Elliott's quiet nature?

Even at the end of an excellent professional-learning session and holidays in the air, there was always something to this job . . . a new set of thoughts weighing on him. Some professional, some personal, but always present. That seemed to be the way it was.

QUESTIONS

1. How should Joe adjust his practice to change the amount of time he spends on management?
2. Evaluate Joe's interaction with Charity Hampton.
3. Evaluate Joe's handling of Dalton Myerly and his computer prank.
4. How should Claire and Joe address their concerns about Elliott's adjustment to life at Pinicon and being the principal's son?

Chapter Seventeen

Mid-December

Looking Back, Looking Ahead

CRUEL AND UNUSUAL PUNISHMENT

McHale had advised Joe to let calls from unrecognized numbers roll over to voicemail after school hours. Joe heeded the advice, but often found himself wondering who was calling and why. "Don't you always make a show of turning your phone off in faculty meetings? I'm not taking second place to your phone, Mr. Gentry. Turn it off," Claire said, passing the salad.

As Joe and Claire were cleaning up the dishes, Margaret scampered off to answer the landline before they could tell her not to. It was Denise Myerly, Dalton's mom. Joe knew divorces were always complicated, and he tried not to let Dave's description of his ex-wife color his perception.

Denise was as pleasant as she could be. She knew Dave had talked with Joe and said the two of them worked hard to be consistent in raising Dalton. "I guess you know that my son is a computer fanatic and not always in a positive way," she laughed.

"He's certainly talented. Like a lot of kids, the key is helping them use it appropriately."

"You may have seen my name on a lot of your supply invoices," she said. "I'm the sales rep for American School Supply. Most of the Pinicon and Kessler supplies come through us."

"Sure! I knew your name was familiar. Aren't we privileged status or something?"

"Yes. You're a premier customer, which means you get 30 percent off just about everything. We're also a yearbook sponsor."

"It goes without saying how much we appreciate it, Denise. I'm sorry we haven't met."

She apologized too and said she had been traveling a lot. She thanked Joe for his quick handling of "Dalton's little prank" and having him take down the wallpaper immediately.

"I am troubled by a couple of things," she said. "I question the scare tactics with talk about police and legal stuff. And telling him you're gonna have some Kessler kids beat him up? That sounds like adult bullying to me."

Joe said he was trying to help Dalton understand that his prank was serious. "I see kids over and over who don't think about any real-world consequences, so I tried to help him see that. I certainly didn't say I was going to have anyone beat him up. That would be completely unprofessional and not something I would do. I did tell him some kids might be offended and that I can't control what happens outside of school."

"Well, that's not what he told me. He said you could say the word and those Kessler kids would beat him up," she said with a much sharper tone. "Saturday School is cruel and unusual punishment for something so harmless. And I don't appreciate you playing good ol' boys with my ex-husband while he trashes my reputation." Joe said that Dave had merely stopped in the office, but it was to no avail. She was not listening.

"We have family tickets to the Invention Convention in Detroit this weekend. We're leaving Friday morning, so Dalton will not be serving Saturday School." Joe explained that if he missed Saturday School, he would be suspended for two days at school.

"That's absolutely ridiculous," Denise snapped. "It's probably also ridiculous to have a school like Pinicon getting the premier discount on our products, no more than you buy. And we should reevaluate our sponsorship of the yearbook. My manager has been after me for both of those things for a long time now."

Margaret was walking a Barbie doll up his leg, indicating it was time to play school and Joe had heard enough. "Denise, know that we appreciate the discount and service we get from you and your company. I don't see Dalton as a bad kid. He made a mistake. We're dealing with it and moving on. Our policy on Saturday School and suspension is what it is. We hope you will support us."

"I'm a strong supporter of the school and my son, which is why we're going to the Invention Convention and he will be unable to come to Saturday School," she said, more calmly.

"I'm glad I could explain the policy because it doesn't leave me a lot of flexibility."

"I understand. In the same way shrinking margins and my manager don't allow me much flexibility on maintaining the discount and yearbook sponsorship."

"I appreciate the call, Denise. Thank you for letting me know, and have a safe trip to Detroit," Joe said, a little more pointedly than he had intended.

ON THE ROAD AT PIEDMONT

Soft-spoken Javaris Hayes was a model student and gifted athlete. He rarely said anything and when he did, his words were concise and spoken in a soft tone. He never missed school events, whether he was a performer or spectator. Whatever the activity, Javaris was there, often with his family in tow.

Joe was surprised when Javaris and two other members of the varsity basketball team walked into his office before 8:00 on a Wednesday morning. "Can we see you a minute?" Javaris asked, standing quietly in the doorway as his teammates looked on.

"Absolutely, fellas. Come on in. Sorry we missed the game at Piedmont last night. Sounds like a tough one to lose. What's up?"

Javaris looked at his teammates, Ben Prior and Heath Farstad. Ben, the son of math teacher Rhonda Prior, spoke first. "There was some crazy stuff going on that we figured you should know about. Maybe you already do," Ben said.

"All I know is that it's a rivalry game. What kind of stuff are you talking about?"

Heath spoke. "Their fans. Some of it was normal crowd stuff, but a lot was personal. Like they had researched guys' families. They were talking about guys' sisters and moms and stuff."

"You mean chanting? Profanity?" Joe asked.

"No, this was all quieter, like when we were taking the ball out of bounds. Just loud enough that you could hear when you were on that end of the floor or close to them."

Ben spoke next. "The regular stuff I can handle and so can my mom. But a lot of it was racist and about Javaris and the other guys. And they were all dressed up."

The boys said the Piedmont student section was dressed in all sorts of costumes, from superheroes to movie characters and random masks. "A bunch of them had their faces painted black, and those guys were wearing our guys' numbers. Our black guys, I mean," Ben said. They made all kinds of noises whenever Javaris and the guys had the ball."

"What kind of noises?" Joe asked.

Ben hesitated. "Like animal sounds. Monkeys and stuff."

Joe asked a few more questions and jotted a few notes. They said Tim Lang, the Pinicon coach, had complained to the referees. They heard the public address announcer remind fans to refrain from using profanity and throwing things on the court. Beyond that, they said not much was done. As the boys left his office, Joe regretted staying home for Elliott's freshman game (which he had thoroughly enjoyed) and not going to Piedmont to watch the varsity (which felt like his duty) since Young was out of town at a conference.

Joe interrupted Rhonda Prior's homeroom to ask what she had seen. "In seventeen years here, Joe, I've never seen anything like it. What they did to our kids made me sick. School spirit and having fun are fine, but this was mean and hurtful. They were mocking our Kessler kids, and it was way over the line. I even got into it with a parent."

"Did their AD or principal do anything?"

"They said something on the PA, but it didn't help. We were sitting across from their students, so we couldn't hear what they were saying, but you could tell by the noises and the face paint that they were way out of line."

Joe asked her to email him a thorough description of what she had seen and left a message with Coach Lang, who taught at the elementary building, to call him immediately. By ten o'clock, Joe had talked with most of the parents who had attended the game, including Susan Shottenkirk.

"It's just a bad place. I'm surprised Frank Young didn't arrange for you or someone to be there, given all the history," Susan said. "They were really crude, but that's Piedmont."

"I appreciate the information and the history, Susan." Joe said.

"As bad as it was, some of our boys didn't help much," Susan added.

"What do you mean?"

"Well, I know all the coaches talk about mental toughness. Frankly, a lot of our boys forgot that. Especially the Kessler ones."

Joe had grown tired of people referring to former Kessler students as though they still went there, but he knew who she was talking about.

"I mean, if Javaris is such a gifted athlete, he has to expect some taunting. It's the price for all the accolades and attention. You block it out and go on. You certainly don't spit at them or grab your crotch in response. That just made it worse."

Joe wondered if the Pinicon players had contributed, but no one else reported seeing anything. Gene DeVore, who rarely missed a Pinicon game, said, "It was really terrible what they did to those boys, especially to the new boys from Kessler. Some of it was downright racial, with all the face painting and so on." It was the first time Joe had spoken to DeVore since his concern about the poetry unit in Allison Jesup's class. If DeVore had any lingering frustration, he hid it. He was gracious and friendly, and seemed as though he had moved on.

Coach Lang said he would have pulled his team off the floor if he had heard any racial comments. "I've really watched for that, Joe. It was crazy in there, but I didn't see our guys do anything to retaliate. We talked about it before the game and they knew my expectations."

PRINCIPALS SUPPORTING PRINCIPALS?

Joe was unsure of what to do. He was content to hand it off to Young, but McHale said it rose to the principal's level and Young was out of town anyway. Professor Summers agreed and said, "It's a good example of how anything can ultimately involve the principal, even with a good AD." Both suggested Joe call the Piedmont principal, Fred Pruitt.

The call did not go well. Pruitt said he enjoyed "seeing both teams really get after each other." When Joe brought up the Piedmont fans' behavior, he was unresponsive. "Joe, I know you're new to this, but you're not new to basketball. This is a rivalry game, hotly contested. I didn't hear or see anything inappropriate. I'm not sure what the problem is."

Joe summarized the consistent story that he had collected: that Piedmont students were unruly and disrespectful, but in race-based ways that went unaddressed. "The straw that broke the camel's back, Fred, is the face paint. The simple fact is that your kids being in blackface wearing our guys' numbers is a racial slur. A taunt."

Pruitt paused for several seconds. "Joe, I don't know what to tell you. We work hard at sportsmanship. I can assure you, there was no racial or racist intent. Our colors are black and red. Kids have dressed up for the Pinicon game for as long as I can remember. It's not about your *black kids*. It's about our school colors. And your kids have plenty of swagger. A little cocky."

"Fred, that's an easy thing to say as a fifty-year-old white guy. I'm not calling anyone racist but when our kids see yours raising hell, faces painted black, *wearing Javaris Hayes's number*, and making jungle noises, how are they supposed to take it? What am I missing?"

"Maybe there should have been some Pinicon administration present," Young inserted.

Joe pushed on, ignoring the jab. "If you didn't hear it, you didn't hear it. But it's an issue for us. I think it needs to be discussed at the conference principals' meeting."

"I've got no problem with that. But I'm not about to do anything that kills Piedmont school spirit," he said. "I think we can get . . . what should I say . . . overly sensitive these days."

Joe sensed that he should quit, but didn't. "Fred, this is not being overly sensitive about healthy high school competition. It's wrong."

"I appreciate the heads-up. I really do. You're new to the rivalry, but we can talk about that at the principals' meeting, huh?" Pruitt offered.

His words were fine. It was the tone that was condescending.

"I appreciate the time, Fred."

A FAILED IDEA?

Margaret Gentry could barely contain her excitement. Joe had promised for a few weeks to take the family to an indoor water park for a pre-Christmas getaway. Young and Den Herder had arrangements for six students assigned to Saturday School during the Pirate Invitational Wrestling Tournament, which was larger than usual. That meant extra healthy gate and concession receipts for the school and Pirate Booster Club.

The call from Young came a little after 7:00 on Saturday night. "I hate to bother you on your getaway, but I knew you'd want to know," he began. Because of the tournament's record numbers, the gate would be much higher than normal, pushing $5,000.

"Holy Toledo! That's big money for a wrestling meet! Awesome," Joe said, eyes wide.

"The bad news is that we're about $3,500 short of that," Young said.

He explained that he had been getting teams settled, handling late officials, and jump-starting a school bus and fell behind on depositing gate money in the safe. "The first $1,500 made it to the safe because Susan Shottenkirk and I counted it and put it there, but the rest is missing—*all* of the afternoon gate receipts. I've talked to Den Herder, Susan, all the coaches, and most of the parents who worked concessions. Nobody remembers anyone messing around the supply room, but there were a ton of people in and out of there. Including the Saturday School kids."

"Den Herder has no idea? Wasn't he watching them?" Joe asked.

"Yeah, but he got pulled into weigh-ins and other stuff. It was just crazy here, Joe, but the kids were great. In fact, I was gonna call to tell you how well they did. I can't believe it was the biggest tournament we've ever had and I managed to lose all of the goddamn gate money."

"*You* didn't lose anything. Have you called the cops?"

"Not yet. Of course everyone is fingering the Saturday School kids," Young said.

"I'm sure they are. Maybe that's why they enjoyed helping," Joe sighed. "You better call Lieutenant Beckworth and get him started."

"I know you thought you should be here for the tournament and I said go, we can handle it. I guess I was wrong, Joe. I'm really sorry. Helluva Christmas present I've given you."

"Listen, Frank. Not another word of apology. It's not your fault. End of discussion."

Claire saw from across the pool deck that something was up and a cloud had arrived over their outing. Joe's furrowed brow gave it away. It always seemed to be something. After Joe explained what had happened, she grabbed the beach towel out of his hand, pulled him toward the line for the waterslide, and said, "Control what you can control, Mr. Gentry."

COLD CASE

On Monday morning Joe stopped by the Pinicon Police Department to see if Beckworth could share anything about the investigation. "You'll have this solved in a half hour, just like on TV, right, Marty?" he asked the lieutenant.

Beckworth sensed Joe's frustration. "You've gotta depersonalize it. Cops have the same problem. We want to catch the bad guy and take it personal when we don't. I've done several interviews and checked the video, but nothing so far. Might be the perfect crime. Too damn many people and confusion. We're talking a class D felony, a zillion potential thieves, but dead ends right now," he said. "I'll go as deep as I can and hopefully make someone sweat a little, but sometimes the best we can do is send a message. They may slide by this time, but not every time. Eventually, I'm gonna win. I'll keep you posted."

Joe's phone chirped on his way back to school. Zylstra.

"Sorry to hear about the mess at the tournament, Joe," she said. "Any leads?"

"I just left the cop shop. Nothing. Frank Young is just sick over it."

"I know. And I know there's a lot of finger pointing. I think Saturday School is a great idea and I fully support it, but FYI, some board members are not as enlightened. I've told them what happened and that there's an investigation, but a few already knew. Word travels fast."

"And what are they saying?" Joe asked.

Zylstra said a couple board members seemed very understanding and knew that this was the biggest tournament in years. "One of them was there and said it was the best-run tournament he'd seen. A couple of others wondered about why Saturday School kids were working around the money. I wondered if they had gotten a call from Susan Shottenworth."

"Shotten*kirk*," Joe corrected.

"Right. Whatever."

"You know those Saturday School kids are there for things like tardies and detentions, right? We're not talking hardened criminals or Hell's Angels."

"I know. Just be ready to tell the board how and why you implemented it, how it was staffed, and so on. Sometimes boards start micromanaging because a member wants to be the hero. I'm going to try to cut that off," she said. "I'm sorry this mess came up right before the holidays. The timing is no good, but maybe it will blow over during break."

Joe thanked her and said he would be glad to speak to the board. Rumors dominated the day and much of the final week before winter break. Some were certain the Saturday School kids were responsible. Others suspected wrestlers or concession stand volunteers. Don Mitchell called to remind Joe that the students responsible for the homecoming mischief had also never been caught. "You and that cop have got to nail somebody for credibility's sake," he warned. "You've got to show that they can't get away with it."

McHALE'S DIRECTIVE

"I don't think I've ever been more ready for a breather," Joe said, relaxing in McHale's office just after school had dismissed for winter break.

"I can imagine. I heard you say there wasn't time to see your friends Sutt and Kristi over break and I know how close you are. You need to spend some time together," McHale said, sliding a $100 gift card across the table. "Let me cover some of the gas, appetizers, or drinks."

Joe protested. "Tom, that's really thoughtful of you, but—"

He held his hand up in front of Joe. "As your mentor, I ask questions, offer advice, but let you decide. This time, I'm not asking. I'm *telling*," he said.

When Joe presented McHale's directive, Sutt and Kristi agreed that they should make time to meet. Although there were other, closer potential meeting spots, Kristi insisted they gather back at the Northgate Grill. To say it was refreshing to reunite with his confidants was an understatement.

"My God, it's like not seeing your kids for a couple of weeks! You guys have grown!" Sutt said laughingly.

"Grown, we have," Kristi agreed.

And they were off, filling the afternoon with reflections, frustrations, stories, and questions. Kristi's eyes welled with tears as she described a first-grade boy who brought a 9 millimeter to school to hide it from his mom's abusive boyfriend. She hoped Child Protective Services would quickly find him a foster home. "I was physically sick when I heard the whole story. He was trying to do the right thing. School is the safest place he knows."

Joe said he was preparing to speak to the school board about the missing money from the wrestling tournament. "I give pretty standard reports at board meetings, but this will be a little different. Plus, Don Mitchell, the associate super, has been on my case about why the Pinicon police and I haven't solved this and the homecoming pranks."

He also shared his uncertainty over what would happen at the next principals meeting when he planned to call on his colleagues to examine fan behavior after the Pinicon-Piedmont basketball game.

"The activities can be a killer," Sutt agreed. "Last week, I had a kid arrested for throwing a frozen Coke bottle at the girls' basketball bus from Fort Reynolds High. Chucked it off the overpass and damn near sent the bus into the ditch. And then there's the parents. I had a couple threaten to sue me because they think I caused their daughter's eating disorder."

"I'll tell you what, I'm ready for Christmas break," Kristi said.

"That would be *winter* break, Ms. Peters," Sutt said and laughed.

"Good to know you're politically correct," said Joe.

"I wasn't the other day at the district principals meeting. Rudy had the flu, so I presented some of his new ideas. I got finished and a junior high principal said something about Rudy being more style than substance. I just said he should come to the building and look around."

"Great restraint," Joe said.

"Yeah, but then he said, 'We've done things this way for a long time, son.' The dude called me *son*."

"Oh, God," Kristi sighed. "I'm afraid to ask what happened next."

"I said, 'Maybe it's time to look at something new, *old-timer*.' I was through listening to his bullshit and wanted to stick up for Rudy and the building. The curriculum director stepped in and went on with things. I don't think I have to take that, but I'm probably in trouble again."

Kristi refocused the group. "We could trade stories all afternoon, but I want to talk about things that have gone well and what we want to focus on when we get back in January."

"Always the taskmaster," Sutt said.

"I'll go first," she said. "I think I'm getting better at seeing other people's perspectives and anticipating things. Like that teacher who fell asleep in my opening meeting. He really thinks I was trying to humiliate him by calling him out. And when my teachers came back from that conference wanting to buy that leadership program, but I wanted to develop our own. Developing a thick skin is important, but so is not being rattled by the unexpected stuff."

"What you're really talking about is anticipating things that can't be anticipated," Joe said.

Sutt spoke next. "My biggest success actually comes from being a shop teacher. I've spent my whole life messing around with things—tools, engines, woodworking. If I do it long enough, I can usually figure it out. I was intimidated at first because I've *just been a shop teacher*, but messing around and giving things a try, like the writing center, helps. I don't mind if it takes a while. We'll eventually get it. I've surprised myself that way."

Joe smiled. "I can't point to any one thing. My teachers might be tired of it, but I'm glad I realized that the Pinicon Way needs defining. And they're responding pretty well. Giving teachers time to talk about big issues has been good. We've spent a lot of time on messy stuff like philosophy. It's frustrating at times, but I think they agree that it's an investment, especially after our last faculty meeting when they thanked me for the opportunity."

They spent the next twenty minutes building upon lessons learned before Kristi turned their attention to what each hoped to improve upon when school resumed. "I really want to focus on building trust. I can tie just about everything back to that—the sleeping teacher, wanting to develop our own student leadership and discipline program. I'm doing okay with management, but I thought once that was under control I would magically jump to the big stuff, like instructional leadership. Now I know it's more complicated than that. Trust has to happen first and I'm not quite there."

"My trust issue relates to trusting *myself.* I need to lean less on Rudy," Sutt said. "He's really supportive, but I go to him for affirmation too much. He's never really redirected me, except when I pissed off the maintenance guy. I've got more confidence that I can help teachers grow and I'm not just a shoppy in the office. I need to be me, but if I'm going to really help teachers, I know I have to polish my approach a little. I know I come off a little too rough sometimes. So it's confidence and the way I present myself."

Joe was next. "Everything you said applies to me, too. I can fit everything under defining the Pinicon Way—our culture, expectations of each other and kids, the way we teach. I hope a common definition will help with my conflicts with Petersen, Patrazzo, and Charity Hampton, but building trust and polishing my approach is a big part of it, too. And I know it takes time. We also need to start looking at *real evidence* for how we're doing. Pinicon's a good school, but I don't think teachers have looked at evidence before."

"It's funny. We have such different circumstances, but similar goals," Kristi said.

"Jeez. I almost forgot," Joe inserted. "Balance. Truth is, that should probably be my biggest goal. Claire has called me out a few times. I knew it would be an adjustment for the whole family, but I didn't realize how much. I don't have it figured out, but I'm working on it."

"Forgetting to bring it up might prove there's a problem, huh, Joe?" Kristi teased. "But I have to watch that too, because it seems like some people *expect* me to work all the time, since I don't have a family and I'm a woman. And in a lot of cases, that's exactly what I do, but I know it's not a good idea for the long term."

Joe nodded. "I know. Dr. Zylstra always talks about balance and the time it takes to build trust and capacity, but she's not my supervisor—Don Mitchell is. And he wants to meet soon to do my midyear evaluation. Instead of balance and time, all I get from him is second-guessing and pressure to figure out who did the homecoming vandalism and stole the money from the wrestling tournament. That stuff is on my mind way too much, not to mention what to do with my teacher headaches, Mace Stallworth's special-ed situation, and how to keep Robin Stiles from falling through the mental-health cracks."

"What weighs on you the most?" Sutt asked. "The issues or the evaluation?"

"All of the above. I don't have much confidence in Mitchell, but he's the one doing my eval, so we'll see. I've never been nervous about being evaluated before. I'm not sure why this time."

Sutt nodded. "I know. There's always more work to do and I can't turn it off when I go home. You don't just forget about a girl like Robin at five o'clock. The issues weigh on my mind, *plus* whether people think I'm handling them right. That shit can be overwhelming. Rudy has this thing he calls *dropping it off.* He made me find a place I pass on the way home where I mentally drop all the school stuff off to clear my head. Mine is an old warehouse by the river. I try to leave everything there and pick it up in the morning. It sounds crazy, but it kind of works for me."

"I like the idea of mentally dropping it off somewhere. I'm gonna try that," Joe said.

"And beyond the mental stuff, I'm glad your mentor forced us to get together. It's good just to be somewhere else. To change the scenery. I've got a million things waiting for me when school starts again, but they'll be there whether I'm refreshed or not, so I might as well take care of myself. I need to get away mentally and physically more often," Sutt said.

"Right. Things like my eval and the stuff hanging over my head feel heavy because I've let them occupy more of my mind than they deserve. I remember Summers warning that school leadership would consume as much of us as we allow it to. Man, that's the truth," Joe said.

"So what about job satisfaction? Ever think of going back to the classroom?" Kristi asked.

"Sometimes it's a love-hate relationship. I love the chance to make a difference, but hate some of what I have to go through to get the chance. I've had my moments, but honestly, I'm having a ball," Sutt said. "There's a lot of wacko stuff, but that's what keeps it fresh. And sharing it with you two makes all the difference."

"No doubt. We have to know that anything can happen, but still be able to lead when it does," Joe said. "And I love the challenge, even when it's trying to fix something I should have done differently. Don't get me wrong, that missing money, Mitchell's eval, and the other stuff I've told you about are looming and I'm gonna savor every minute of this break, but I'm looking forward to the second half of the year."

Nodding their agreement, they noticed a tough-looking old man in a sweatshirt rising from his barstool behind them. He pulled on a flannel-lined work coat and cap and walked over to their table. "Pardon the interruption," he said. "I stopped in here for a sandwich and was taken with your conversation. Wasn't trying to eavesdrop, but it's fascinating and I couldn't leave."

Sutt laughed. "What you heard just scratched the surface. There's more where that came from."

"I know. I used to be a principal. Twenty-eight years," he said. "Of course, it's different now with the emphasis on tests, more social problems, the media, you name it. If I hadn't been one, I'd wonder who in the hell wants the job. I'd love to know how all of this turns out for you three."

The young principals laughed. "We wish we knew. If you come back here in June, we'll be able to tell you," Kristi offered.

"I hope so. I'm glad there are folks like you stepping up to the job. You can't make this stuff up, but the opportunity for an impact is irreplaceable," the slight old man said as he tipped his plaid cap and headed into the December snow. "Hope to see you then."

QUESTIONS

1. Evaluate Joe's conversation with Denise Myerly.
2. Assess Joe's response to events at the Piedmont basketball game and his interaction with Fred Pruitt.
3. How should Joe proceed on the missing money, Saturday School, and the school board's questions?
4. What strengths and growth areas do you see for Sutt, Kristi, and Joe at the midway point in their first year?
5. How should Joe prepare for the midyear evaluation with Don Mitchell?
6. What issues are the most intriguing for the second half of Joe's first year as principal?

References

Barth, R. S. (2006). Improving relationships within the schoolhouse. *Educational Leadership* *63*(6), 8–13.

Bolman, L. G., & Deal, T. E. (2008). *Reframing organizations: Artistry, choice, and leadership* (4th ed.). San Francisco: Jossey-Bass.

Fullan, M. (2008). *What's worth fighting for in the principalship* (2nd ed.). New York: Teachers College Press.

Horwitz, T. (1998). *Confederates in the attic: Dispatches from the unfinished Civil War*. New York: Pantheon Books.

O' Brien, T. (1990). *The things they carried*. New York: Houghton Mifflin Harcourt.

Pace, N. J. (2009). *The principal's challenge: Learning from gay and lesbian students*. Charlotte, NC: Information Age.

Pace, N. J. (2011). *The principal's hot seat: Observing real-world dilemmas*. Lanham, MD: Rowman & Littlefield Education.

Scott, S. (2004). *Fierce conversations: Achieving success at work and in life, one conversation at a time*. New York: Berkley Books.

Whitaker, T. (2004). *What great teachers do differently: Fourteen things that matter most*. Larchmont, NY: Eye on Education.

79028761R00121

Made in the USA
Lexington, KY
17 January 2018